BIBLE STUDY GUIDE

From the Bible-teaching ministry of

INSIGHT FOR LIVING

Charles R. Swindoll is a graduate of Dallas Theological Seminary and has served in pastorates for more than twenty-three years, including churches in Texas, New England, and California. Since 1971 he has served as senior pastor of the First Evangelical Free Church of Fullerton, California. Chuck's radio program, "Insight for Living," began in 1979. In addition to his church and radio ministries, Chuck has written twenty-one books and numerous booklets on a variety of subjects.

Based on the outlines of Chuck's sermons, the study guide text is coauthored by Ken Gire, Jr., a graduate of Texas Christian University and Dallas Theological Seminary. The Living Insights are written by Bill Butterworth, a graduate of Florida Bible College, Dallas Theological Seminary, and Florida Atlantic University. Ken Gire, Jr., is presently the director of educational products at Insight for Living, and Bill Butterworth is currently the director of counseling ministries.

Editor in Chief:	Cynthia Swindoll
Coauthor of Text:	Ken Gire, Jr.
Author of Living Insights:	Bill Butterworth
Editorial Assistant:	Julie Martin
Copy Manager:	Jac La Tour
Senior Copy Assistant:	Jane Gillis
Copy Assistant:	Wendy Peterson
Director, Communications Division:	Carla Beck
Project Manager:	Nina Paris
Art Director:	Becky Englund
Production Artists:	Karen Hall and Donna Mayo
Typographer:	Bob Haskins
Calligrapher:	David Acquistapace
Cover:	Painting by Heinrich Hofmann, *Jesus among the Doctors in the Temple*
Print Production Manager:	Deedee Snyder
Printer:	Frye and Smith

Ordering Information

An album that contains eight messages on four cassettes and corresponds to this study guide may be purchased through Insight for Living, Post Office Box 4444, Fullerton, California 92634. For ordering information and a current catalog, please write our office or call (714) 870-9161.

Canadian residents may obtain a catalog and ordering information through Insight for Living Ministries, Post Office Box 2510, Vancouver, British Columbia, Canada V6B 3W7, (604) 272-5811. Overseas residents should direct their correspondence to our Fullerton office.

If you wish to order by Visa or MasterCard, you are welcome to use our toll-free number, (800) 772-8888, Monday through Friday between the hours of 8:30 A.M. and 4:00 P.M., Pacific time. This number may be used anywhere in the continental United States except Alaska, California, and Hawaii. Orders from these areas can be made by calling our general office number, (714) 870-9161. Orders from Canada can be made by calling (604) 272-5811.

Table of Contents

Jesus, Our Lord

Jesus.

There is no greater name. He alone deserves our highest praise, our constant devotion, our daily obedience. Why? Because He alone is Lord.

These studies will turn our attention to Him. If you look over the table of contents, you will discover that one study follows another, tracing Christ's life in chronological order. So, we will be journeying through the New Testament with our Lord from His preexistence with the Father to His return to heaven as the ascended Christ.

In a day when the Person of Christ is under such relentless attack by religious cults and secular philosophies, it's necessary that we who are Christians understand what the Bible declares and what it means to follow Jesus as our Lord.

May each study assist you in making that understanding a reality in your life.

Chuck Swindoll

Putting Truth into Action

Knowledge apart from application falls short of God's desire for His children. Knowledge must result in change and growth. Consequently, we have constructed this Bible study guide with these purposes in mind: (1) to stimulate discovery, (2) to increase understanding, and (3) to encourage application.

At the end of each lesson is a section called **Living Insights.** There you'll be given assistance in further Bible study, and you'll be encouraged to contemplate and apply the things you've learned. This is the place where the lesson is fitted with shoe leather for your walk through the varied experiences of life.

It's our hope that you'll discover numerous ways to use this tool. Some useful avenues we suggest are personal meditation, joint discovery, and discussion with your spouse, family, work associates, friends, or neighbors. The study guide is also practical for Sunday school classes, Bible study groups, and, of course, as a study aid for the "Insight for Living" radio broadcast.

In order to derive the greatest benefit from this process, we suggest that you record your responses in a notebook where writing space is plentiful. In view of the kinds of questions asked, your notebook may become a journal filled with your many discoveries and commitments. We anticipate that you will find yourself returning to it periodically for review and encouragement.

Ken Gire, Jr.
Coauthor of Text

Bill Butterworth
Author of Living Insights

Jesus, Our Lord

Jesus: His Existence Before Creation

John 8, Matthew 16

Clive Staples Lewis began his academic career at Oxford as a brilliant and confident young atheist. His anger at a God he no longer believed existed most probably stemmed from a devastating childhood experience. In his impressionable childhood years, Lewis saw his mother dying of cancer. He prayed to God to heal her, but the words, he felt, fell on deaf and distant ears, for just before he turned ten, his mother died.

In the years that followed, Lewis dismissed the existence of a caring, loving God and relegated the Bible to storybook status. As a student, long before he held the chair of Medieval and Renaissance English Literature at Cambridge, his atheism flowered in Oxford's soil. But slowly and certainly, God was uprooting him to shake him free. Lewis resisted, his roots tenaciously clinging, but the pull of God was relentless. In his book *Surprised by Joy,* Lewis gives a vivid account of the battle for his soul. "I was like a man who has lost 'merely a pawn' and never dreams that this (in that state of the game) means mate in a few moves."[1] Describing his anxiety caused by God's pursuit, he states, "The fox had been dislodged from Hegelian Wood and was now running in the open, 'with all the wo in the world,' bedraggled and weary, hounds barely a field behind."[2] He continues with another image, "And so the great Angler played His fish and I never dreamed that the hook was in my tongue."[3] Finally, God dips His net; the fish is still fighting, but the contest is over.

> You must picture me alone in that room in Magdalen, night after night, feeling, whenever my mind lifted even for a second from my work, the steady, unrelenting approach of Him whom I so earnestly desired not to meet. That which I greatly feared had

1. C. S. Lewis, *Surprised by Joy: The Shape of My Early Life* (New York, N.Y.: Harcourt Brace Jovanovich, 1955), p. 222.

2. Lewis, *Surprised by Joy,* p. 225.

3. Lewis, *Surprised by Joy,* p. 211.

at last come upon me. In the Trinity Term of 1929 I gave in, and admitted that God was God, and knelt and prayed: perhaps, that night, the most dejected and reluctant convert in all England. I did not then see what is now the most shining and obvious thing; the Divine humility which will accept a convert even on such terms. The Prodigal Son at least walked home on his own feet. But who can duly adore that Love which will open the high gates to a prodigal who is brought in kicking, struggling, resentful, and darting his eyes in every direction for a chance of escape?[4]

And that night, Jesus became C. S. Lewis's Lord.

I. The Question of Jesus' Identity

Lewis's conversion may not mirror our own, but before we ever come into the family of God, we, like Lewis, must come to grips with the identity of Jesus in a personal, one-on-one encounter. Upon entering Caesarea Philippi, Jesus penetrated His disciples' thinking with a question that forced such an encounter: " 'Who do people say that the Son of Man is?' " (Matt. 16:13). That question echoes as loudly today as it did back then.

   A. Who is Jesus, according to people today? Some say He's a great human teacher . . . the founder of Christianity . . . a Nazarene carpenter's son . . . a Jew who claimed to be the Messiah . . . a first-century martyr who died for a noble cause . . . the Son of God. In his book *Mere Christianity,* Lewis narrows the options to three.

   I am trying here to prevent anyone saying the really foolish thing that people often say about Him: "I'm ready to accept Jesus as a great moral teacher, but I don't accept His claim to be God." That is the one thing we must not say. A man who was merely a man and said the sort of things Jesus said would not be a great moral teacher. He would either be a lunatic— on a level with the man who says he is a poached egg—or else he would be the Devil of Hell. You must make your choice. Either this man was, and is, the Son of God: or else a madman or something worse. You can shut Him up for a fool, you can spit at Him and kill Him as a demon; or you can fall at His feet and call Him Lord and God. But let us not come with any patronising nonsense about His being a great human teacher. He has not left that open to us. He did not intend to.[5]

4. Lewis, *Surprised by Joy,* pp. 228–29.

5. C. S. Lewis, *Mere Christianity,* rev. and enl. (1952; reprint, New York, N.Y.: Macmillan Publishing Co., 1960), pp. 40–41.

B. Who was Jesus, according to the people of the first century? The question begged in the streets of Jerusalem like an impoverished orphan. His disciples asked: " 'Who then is this, that even the wind and the sea obey Him?' " (Mark 4:41). Reporting to Jesus the conclusions of others, His disciples said, " 'Some say John the Baptist; and others, Elijah; but still others, Jeremiah, or one of the prophets' " (Matt. 16:14). The scribes and the Pharisees' applecart of messianic expectations was especially upset by this unsettling preacher from Nazareth: " 'Who is this man who speaks blasphemies?' " (Luke 5:21); " 'Who is this man who even forgives sins?' " (7:49). The persistent question went so far as to knock on the doors of the highest government officials. Herod pondered: " 'I myself had John beheaded; but who is this man about whom I hear such things?' " (9:9). Finally and climactically—face-to-face—Pilate questions Jesus' identity: " 'Are You the King of the Jews?' " (23:3).

C. Who is Jesus, according to His own claim? After His disciples told Jesus who the people thought Him to be, Jesus handed Peter the pointed end of the question.

> He said to them, "But who do *you* say that I am?" And Simon Peter answered and said, "Thou art the Christ, the Son of the living God." And Jesus answered and said to him, "Blessed are you, Simon Barjona, because flesh and blood did not reveal this to you, but My Father who is in heaven." (Matt. 16:15–17, emphasis added)

Jesus' blessing on Peter indicated that He agreed with and approved of Peter's statement. Another disciple, Thomas, gave a similar confession in John 20:26–29. Notice that Jesus did not rebuke Thomas for calling Him God, nor did He rebuke Thomas for falling down to worship Him.[6]

> And after eight days again His disciples were inside, and Thomas with them. Jesus came, the doors having been shut, and stood in their midst, and said, "Peace be with you." Then He said to Thomas, "Reach here your finger, and see My hands; and reach here your

---

6. When Paul healed a lame man at Lystra, the crowd broke into an uproar of adoration, thinking Paul and Barnabas to be gods. The multitudes brought oxen to sacrifice and garlands to place upon their heads. But when Paul and Barnabas heard of this, they tore their robes and rushed out to stop the crowd, saying, " 'Men, why are you doing these things? We are also men of the same nature as you....' " (Acts 14:15a). Even angels refuse the worship of men, as illustrated when John fell down at the feet of an angel in the last chapter of Revelation: "And he said to me, 'Do not do that; I am a fellow servant of yours and of your brethren the prophets and of those who heed the words of this book; worship God' " (Rev. 22:9). When Thomas fell down to worship Christ, however, no such rebuke was given. The worship was accepted.

hand, and put it into My side; and be not unbelieving, but believing." Thomas answered and said to Him, "My Lord and my God!" Jesus said to him, "Because you have seen Me, have you believed? Blessed are they who did not see, and yet believed."

The One Important Question

Boiled down to the basics, the essence of life can be distilled into one question: " 'But who do you say that I am?' " As C. S. Lewis instructed, the answer "a good moral teacher" is not an option. Jesus is either lunatic, liar, or He is Lord. Who do *you* say He is?

II. The Issue of Jesus' Eternality

Turning to John 8, we can almost feel the heat rising from the page as the conflict between Jesus and the Pharisees intensifies.

A. According to Jesus Himself. Even at a distance we can hear the clash of sharp words wielded in fury. As we come closer, we can see the sparks flying from a debate over Jesus' identity.

They answered and said to Him, "Abraham is our father." Jesus said to them, "If you are Abraham's children, do the deeds of Abraham. But as it is, you are seeking to kill Me, a man who has told you the truth, which I heard from God; this Abraham did not do. You are doing the deeds of your father." They said to Him, "We were not born of fornication; we have one Father, even God." Jesus said to them, "If God were your Father, you would love Me; for I proceeded forth and have come from God, for I have not even come on My own initiative, but He sent Me. Why do you not understand what I am saying? It is because you cannot hear My word." (vv. 39–43)

In the following verses, the jabs become more pointed. Jesus lunges for the heart, " 'You are of your father the devil' " (v. 44), and the Pharisees parry a rapier reply, " 'You are a Samaritan and have a demon' " (v. 48). Undaunted, Jesus stands His ground: " 'If anyone keeps My word he shall never see death' " (v. 51). With these words, the Pharisees' attack becomes more determined.

The Jews said to Him, "Now we know that You have a demon. Abraham died, and the prophets also; and You say, 'If anyone keeps My word, he shall never taste of death.' Surely You are not greater than our father Abraham, who died? The prophets died too;

whom do You make Yourself out to be?" Jesus answered, ... "Your father Abraham rejoiced to see My day, and he saw it and was glad." The Jews therefore said to Him, "You are not yet fifty years old, and have You seen Abraham?" (vv. 52–54, 56–57)

Jesus then disarms his aggressors with a claim that, to them, was not only bold and brash but blasphemous as well.

Jesus said to them, "Truly, truly, I say to you, before Abraham was born, I am." (v. 58)[7]

When Jesus referred to Himself as "I am," He was not only asserting His supremacy over Abraham and over time, but He was also asserting His identity with God. When God commissioned Moses as His spokesman and leader of His people, Moses asked how he should reply if the people questioned him regarding the identity of the One who sent him. God's response was this: "And God said to Moses, 'I AM WHO I AM'; and He said, 'Thus you shall say to the sons of Israel, "I AM has sent me to you" ' " (Exod. 3:14). So, when Jesus used this designation of deity to refer to Himself, the Pharisees were outraged because they perceived His words as blasphemy.

Therefore they picked up stones to throw at Him; but Jesus hid Himself, and went out of the temple. (v. 59)

According to the Law, blasphemy against God's name warranted death by stoning (Lev. 24:16). Later, in John 10, the Jews took up stones to kill Jesus for the same reason: "The Jews answered Him, 'For a good work we do not stone You, but for blasphemy; and because You, being a man, make Yourself out to be God' " (v. 33).

Lewis on Jesus' Claim to Deity

"Among these Jews there suddenly turns up a man who goes about talking as if He was God.... He says He has always existed.... Among Pantheists ... anyone might say that he was a part of God, or one with God: there would be nothing very odd about it. But this man, since He was a Jew, could not mean that kind of God. God, in their language, meant the Being outside the world Who had made it and was infinitely different from anything else. And when you have grasped that, you will see that what this man said was, quite simply, the most shocking thing that has ever been uttered by human lips."[8]

---

7. Three times in John 8 "I am" is used in the absolute sense (vv. 24, 28, 58). In none of these passages does the third personal pronoun "he" follow the "I am" in the Greek text.

8. Lewis, *Mere Christianity*, p. 40.

B. According to John's Gospel. The eternality of Christ is asserted not only by Himself but also by His closest disciple— the disciple whom Christ loved—John.

> In the beginning was the Word, and the Word was with God, and the Word was God. (John 1:1)

The identity of this *Word* is revealed in verses 14–18.

> And the Word became flesh, and dwelt among us, and we beheld His glory, glory as of the only begotten from the Father, full of grace and truth. John bore witness of Him, and cried out, saying, "This was He of whom I said, 'He who comes after me has a higher rank than I, for He existed before me.'" For of His fulness we have all received, and grace upon grace. For the Law was given through Moses; grace and truth were realized through Jesus Christ. No man has seen God at any time; the only begotten God, who is in the bosom of the Father, He has explained Him.

The *Word* is Jesus Christ. Like a translator teaching someone a foreign language, Jesus explained God to us, translating Him into words we could understand. Jesus could do this because He was not only with God, but He *was* God.[9]

Explaining God

One way that Jesus explained an infinite God to finite human beings was to do the same thing we do with our children—tell them stories. Stories like the prodigal son in Luke 15. One thing we learn about God from this story is that when we return to Him—as C. S. Lewis did—God doesn't wag a critical finger in our face ... doesn't call us names ... doesn't preach. What He does do is wait. He waits on the porch, heart aching for reunion, ears eager for the sound of our voice, eyes searching the horizon for our return. And when we do, He leaps to His feet, and with open arms runs to welcome us home (v. 20). Is that how you view God? If it isn't, maybe somewhere down the line you listened to the wrong stories—or the wrong storyteller.

C. According to Paul's letters. In Philippians 2:5–7, Paul affirms the teaching of John about Christ's deity and incarnation.

9. The Greek word translated *with* means "face-to-face." "Probably we should understand from the preposition the two ideas of accompaniment and relationship.... Not only did the Word exist 'in the beginning', but He existed in the closest possible connection with the Father." Leon Morris, *The Gospel According to John* (Grand Rapids, Mich.: William B. Eerdmans Publishing Co., 1971), p. 76.

Have this attitude in yourselves which was also in Christ Jesus, who, although He existed in the form of God, did not regard equality with God a thing to be grasped, but emptied Himself, taking the form of a bond-servant, and being made in the likeness of men.

In another letter, Paul again agrees with John—that Jesus not only existed before creation, but that "all things came into being by Him, and apart from Him nothing came into being that has come into being" (John 1:3).

For by Him all things were created, both in the heavens and on earth, visible and invisible, whether thrones or dominions or rulers or authorities—all things have been created by Him and for Him. And He is before all things, and in Him all things hold together. (Col. 1:16–17)

III. The Importance of Jesus' Deity

The deity of Jesus is important on two different levels, theological and practical. Theologically, if Jesus isn't eternally God, then the credibility of Scripture is undermined. Practically, if Jesus is a mere man, then He cannot be turned to for help, either for salvation from our sins or for salvation from our day-to-day struggles.

> **A Final Thought from C. S. Lewis**
> "The Son of God became a man to enable men to become sons of God."[10]

 Living Insights

Study One

One of the most fascinating portions of Scripture in this study is the account of Jesus with the Pharisees in John 8. It's not only a fascinating dialogue, but also a very vital passage in understanding Christ's pre-existence.

- Let's zero in on John 8:39–58. As you read through it, you'll observe quite a heated conversation. Can you sense the emotion? Does this true drama come to life for you? Try writing out these verses in your own words. Write expressively. Fill the page with the "heat" that permeates this scene.

Continued on next page

10. Lewis, *Mere Christianity,* p. 139.

Living Insights

The preexistence of Christ may seem to have little or no relevance to your life today. But stop and think about it more carefully. Can you see areas of practicality related to this doctrine?

- Copy the following chart into your notebook. In the left column, write down specific teachings that you gleaned from this study (for example, Christ participated in the Creation, all things are held together by Christ, and so forth). In the right column, write out some personal applications you've drawn from these truths, such as "*every* area of my life is held together by Christ." Think deeply; you may be surprised to discover how much Christ's preexistence does affect your life!

Christ's Existence Before Creation	
Doctrinal Truths	Resulting Applications

Jesus: A Birth Like None Other

Matthew 1, Luke 1

It would be a royal birth—a birth like none other. It would be an event to make the Royal Wedding look like children playing dress-up in the attic; an event to make the Inaugural Ball look like a sock hop in the junior high gym; an event to make the World's Fair look like a small-town flea market.

Yes, it would be a *royal* birth. Invitations would be sent to all national and international dignitaries. Everybody who was anybody would be there. It would be *the* major media event in history. Every network and every newspaper would cover it.

Of course, the royal family would receive the ultimate in VIP treatment: a Rolls Royce limousine for transportation, the Presidential Suite at the finest hotel. For the baby, the most beautiful bassinet money could buy. Satin sheets. A royal wardrobe. The highest quality staff of servants available in the world to attend to the young heir's every coo and cry.

Certainly all the world would stop in reverence for the royal event. Shops would close. Factories would shut down. All transportation and commerce would cease. Every heart would eagerly await this great and glorious birth.

At least, that's how we would have expected the scenario to read. However, the scenario God arranged for the royal birth of His Son reads strangely different. In the latter stages of Mary's pregnancy, the royal family traveled eighty-five miles to Bethlehem to be counted in the national census. Joseph walked; Mary—nine months pregnant—rode sidesaddle on a donkey, feeling every jolt, every rock in the road, every rut. In the small city of Bethlehem, swollen from the influx of travelers, there was no room for them. The inns were packed; the only available accommodation was a stable crowded with the animals of the inn's guests.

In the stable, a feeding trough made do for a crib. Hay served as both mattress and sheets for the young king. Rags used to wipe down the animals were the infant's clothes. Sheep, donkeys, and furtive barn mice were the heir's only attendants. A barnyard stench hung heavy in air that was thick with flies. The stable was dark and dirty—a disquieting place for a woman in the throes of childbirth. Far from home. Far from family. Far from what she expected for her firstborn. Except for Joseph, there was no one to share her pain; no one to share her joy. Yes, there were angels announcing His arrival—but only to a lowly band of blue-collar shepherds. And yes, a magnificent star shone in the sky to mark His birthplace—but only three foreigners bothered to look up and follow it. And thus, in the little town of Bethlehem . . . that one silent night . . . the royal birth of God's only Son tiptoed quietly by . . . as the world slept.

I. The Centrality of Jesus Christ

Without Jesus in the manger, there is no Christianity. Apart from Christ, Christianity is an empty feeding trough, just so much wood and straw. Just as the baby Jesus is the central focus in our nativity scenes, so He should be central in our lives. And just as it's easy to lose the simplicity and purity of Christmas amid the ribbons and bows of the holidays, so it's easy to lose our devotion to Christ amid the tinsel and glitter of life. Paul warns of this danger in 2 Corinthians 11:3.

> But I am afraid, lest as the serpent deceived Eve by his craftiness, your minds should be led astray from the simplicity and purity of devotion to Christ.

Devotion to Christ

The basics. In football, they're blocking and tackling; in baseball, keeping your eye on the ball; in basketball, not giving up the baseline; in the Christian life, devotion to Christ, pure and simple. Oftentimes, when athletes are having trouble with their game, it's because they've gotten away from basics. We're a lot like that in our Christian life—we wander so easily away from the basics. How about your devotion to Christ? Is it pure and simple—like Martha's sister, Mary, who sat attentively at Jesus' feet (Luke 10:39–42)? Or has it been led astray by distractions— as Martha in the kitchen (vv. 40–41)? What about your Christian life? Are you knowing more now but enjoying it less? Maybe you need to get back to the basics—pure and simple devotion to Christ.

II. The Superiority of Jesus Christ

Christ is sufficient for all our needs because of His superiority. He was no ordinary man; He was God. His birth was no ordinary birth; it was a sinless arrival.

A. His divine nature. Jesus is superior to all because He is Creator of all (John 1:3). There was never a time when He did not exist. Before Abraham was, Jesus existed (8:58); before the earth was created, Jesus existed (1:1). Jesus—the same yesterday, today, and forever (Heb. 13:8)—was, is, and forever will be God.

B. His virgin birth. For God to be able to die, He would have to become human. For His death to be an effective atonement for sin, He would have to be sinless. But how was He to become a man without becoming contaminated with sin?

    1. Possibilities at the Father's disposal. *As a first option,* God could have chosen for Jesus to have been born of a good human father and mother. However, the problem with

10

this is that we are all a product of our parentage. David describes the dilemma inherent in natural conception.

Behold, I was brought forth in iniquity,
And in sin my mother conceived me. (Ps. 51:5)

And again in Psalm 58:3.

The wicked are estranged from the womb;
These who speak lies go astray from birth.

An echo of this truth surfaces in Romans 5:12.

Therefore, just as through one man sin entered into the world, and death through sin, and so death spread to all men, because all sinned.

In this option, Jesus would have been all humanity and no deity. *As a second option,* God could have chosen His Son to be created, like an angel, having neither father nor mother. As a created being, He would have been preserved from sin's contamination. But in this case, He would have been all deity and no humanity. *As a third option,* God could have chosen to incarnate the spirit of Christ in a human body, not unlike what is commonly referred to as reincarnation. The problem with this option is that He would not have been fully human in a technical sense. Scripture tells us Jesus had "His own body" and a "body which God prepared for Him." If Christ's spirit had been simply deposited into the body of another, it would not have been His own, thus contradicting the Scriptures. *As a final option,* God could have chosen to select a virgin who, through miraculous conception, could give birth to a child both fully human and fully divine.

2. **Actuality, according to Scripture.** About eight hundred years before Christ, Isaiah stood before King Ahaz and prophesied a special event that would serve as a sign to the nation.

"Therefore the Lord Himself will give you a sign:
Behold, a virgin will be with child and bear a son,
and she will call His name Immanuel." (Isa. 7:14)

In Hebrew the word for *virgin* meant simply "a young maiden."[1] In the Septuagint, the Greek translation of the Hebrew Old Testament, this word was translated into a word meaning "one who had not known another intimately."[2] The translators' understanding of the passage gives a much narrower concept than "a young maiden." A young woman giving birth to a son named Immanuel would hardly qualify as a sign. Instead, this Greek word is used in the New Testament in Luke 1.

1. The Hebrew word is *almah.*
2. The Greek word is *parthenos.*

11

Luke's record is especially valuable, because the facts have been investigated by a physician's careful hand.

> Now in the sixth month the angel Gabriel was sent from God to a city in Galilee, called Nazareth, to a virgin engaged to a man whose name was Joseph, of the descendants of David; and the virgin's name was Mary. (vv. 26–27)

Twice in verse 27 the word *virgin* is used. But it is the broader context of the angel's conversation with Mary that determines its precise meaning. The angel reveals God's unique plan for this favored woman.

> And coming in, he said to her, "Hail, favored one! The Lord is with you." But she was greatly troubled at this statement, and kept pondering what kind of salutation this might be. And the angel said to her, "Do not be afraid, Mary; for you have found favor with God. And behold, you will conceive in your womb, and bear a son, and you shall name Him Jesus. He will be great, and will be called the Son of the Most High; and the Lord God will give Him the throne of His father David; and He will reign over the house of Jacob forever; and His kingdom will have no end." (vv. 28–33)

Her response to this revelation determines the exact meaning of the Greek word translated *virgin*.

> And Mary said to the angel, "How can this be, since I am a virgin?" (v. 34)

In this verse, she literally says, "I know not a man," rather than using the word *virgin*. The clear implication is that she had never known a man intimately, so it would be physically impossible for her to give birth to a child. In response, the angel describes the details of the miracle to her.

> And the angel answered and said to her, "The Holy Spirit will come upon you, and the power of the Most High will overshadow you; and for that reason the holy offspring shall be called the Son of God." (v. 35)

Of course, critics may argue that she was only a virgin at the time of the angel's revelation and later had relations with Joseph that produced the child. However, Matthew 1:18 decisively refutes that theory.

> Now the birth of Jesus Christ was as follows. When His mother Mary had been betrothed to Joseph, before they came together she was found to be with child by the Holy Spirit.

Matthew carefully notes that Mary was pregnant *before* she and Joseph came together. According to Jewish custom, the betrothal period was a twelve-month period of engagement that was an official, binding commitment which could only be broken legally by divorce, or, in the case of unfaithfulness, by death from stoning. The betrothal arrangement was so binding that Joseph was already viewed as Mary's husband.

> And Joseph her husband, being a righteous man, and not wanting to disgrace her, desired to put her away secretly. (v. 19)

Joseph was stunned at the turn of events and found himself in a quandary between conviction and compassion. Interceding on Mary's behalf, however, an angel clarifies the situation to her confused husband.

> But when he had considered this, behold, an angel of the Lord appeared to him in a dream, saying, "Joseph, son of David, do not be afraid to take Mary as your wife; for that which has been conceived in her is of the Holy Spirit. And she will bear a Son; and you shall call His name Jesus, for it is He who will save His people from their sins." (vv. 20–21)

In the next two verses, Matthew comments on this miraculous event, citing it as the sign referred to in Isaiah 7:14.

> Now all this took place that what was spoken by the Lord through the prophet might be fulfilled, saying, "Behold, the virgin shall be with child, and shall bear a Son, and they shall call His name Immanuel," which translated means, "God with us." (vv. 22–23)

Matthew adds a happy postscript to the story:

> And Joseph arose from his sleep, and did as the angel of the Lord commanded him, and took her as his wife, and kept her a virgin until she gave birth to a Son; and he called His name Jesus. (vv. 24–25)

III. The Practicality of It All

The virgin birth has far-reaching ramifications of practical significance. Christianity is Christ. If Christ is only a man, then Christianity is only a human religion. For a natural savior provides no supernatural help, a strictly human savior offers no divine hope, and a sinful savior is really no savior at all.

> **— A Final Application —**
> The fact that there was no room in the inn foreshadowed the Jews' response to Jesus, who "came to His own, and those who were His own did not receive Him" (John 1:11). Now Jesus stands at another door—the door to your heart:
>
> " 'Behold, I stand at the door and knock; if anyone hears My voice and opens the door, I will come in to him, and will dine with him, and he with Me.' "
> (Rev. 3:20)
>
> What about your heart? Is there room? Maybe you've received Him, but the place you've given Him is the stable. If you really believe Jesus is God, shouldn't you offer Him the Presidential Suite instead?

 Living Insights

Study One ▬▬▬▬▬▬▬▬▬▬▬▬▬▬▬▬▬▬▬▬▬▬▬▬▬▬▬▬▬▬▬▬▬▬▬▬▬▬

When we speak of the virgin birth of Christ, we often gloss over it as we think of the familiar Christmas story. When was the last time you really *studied* the birth of Christ? Let's take some time for that now.

- The Christmas story centers on Matthew and Luke's accounts. Spend some time in both passages and jot down significant observations in your notebook. Look especially for facts that are in Matthew but not in Luke, and vice versa.

 Living Insights

Study Two ▬▬▬▬▬▬▬▬▬▬▬▬▬▬▬▬▬▬▬▬▬▬▬▬▬▬▬▬▬▬▬▬▬▬▬▬▬▬

The virgin birth of Christ *guarantees* supernatural help and divine hope. Have you thought of the implications of denying the virgin birth? Let's think through some of the conclusions drawn from the study. Bring together family or close friends and discuss the following:

- *A natural savior provides no supernatural help.* Why? What is "supernatural help"? Why is it significant?
- *A human savior offers no divine hope.* Why? Define "divine hope." How does hope relate to our everyday lives?
- *A sinful savior is really no savior at all.* Why? Which Scriptures support the need for a sinless savior? Review the practical significance of Christ's virgin birth.

Jesus: His God-Man Lifestyle
John 1, Philippians 2:5-7

The Incarnation is what C. S. Lewis called "the Grand Miracle" of Christianity. It is "the central chapter" of a novel, upon which the whole plot turns.

> The story of the Incarnation is the story of a descent and resurrection. . . . I am talking of this whole, huge pattern of descent, down, down, and then up again. . . . The coming down, not only into humanity, but into those nine months which precede human birth . . . and going lower still into being a corpse. . . . One has a picture of a strong man trying to lift a very big, complicated burden. He stoops down and gets himself right under it so that he himself disappears; and then he straightens his back and moves off with the whole thing swaying on his shoulders. Or else one has the picture of a diver, stripping off garment after garment, making himself naked, then flashing for a moment in the air, and then down through the green, and warm, and sunlit water into the pitch black, cold, freezing water, down into the mud and slime, then up again, his lungs almost bursting, back again to the green and warm and sunlit water, and then at last out into the sunshine, holding in his hand the dripping thing he went down to get. This thing is human nature; but, associated with it, all nature, the new universe.[1]

I. A Definition: The Meaning of the Incarnation
In simplest terms, the Incarnation is the union of God and man in the person of Jesus Christ. This union took place at the moment of conception when both natures melded, inseparable, yet unmixed (Luke 1:31-35). In this mysterious union, undiminished deity was veiled in untainted humanity. Coequal, coeternal, and coexistent with the Father, Jesus was both fully God and fully man.[2] In the Incarnation, God dived down into the depths of creation and became a man.[3]

> In the beginning was the Word, and the Word was with God, and the Word was God. . . . And the Word became flesh, and dwelt among us, and we beheld His glory, glory as of the only begotten from the Father, full of grace and truth. (John 1:1, 14; compare 2 Cor. 5:19)

1. C. S. Lewis, *God in the Dock: Essays on Theology and Ethics* (Grand Rapids, Mich.: William B. Eerdmans Publishing Co., 1970), p. 82.

2. The root of the word *incarnation* means "flesh." Chile con *carne* is literally "chile with flesh" or "chili with meat." Incarnation is the act of becoming "in flesh" or embodied.

3. For more information, see L. Berkhof's *Systematic Theology* (Grand Rapids, Mich.: William B. Eerdmans Publishing Co., 1969), pp. 333-36.

The First Real Man

"Did you ever think, when you were a child, what fun it would be if your toys could come to life? Well suppose you could really have brought them to life. Imagine turning a tin soldier into a real little man. It would involve turning the tin into flesh. And suppose the tin soldier did not like it. He is not interested in flesh; all he sees is that the tin is being spoilt. He thinks you are killing him. He will do everything he can to prevent you. He will not be made into a man if he can help it.

What you would have done about that tin soldier I do not know. But what God did about us was this. The Second Person in God, the Son, became human Himself: was born into the world as an actual man—a real man of a particular height, with hair of a particular colour, speaking a particular language, weighing so many [pounds]. The Eternal Being, who knows everything and who created the whole universe, became not only a man but (before that) a baby, and before that a *foetus* inside a Woman's body. If you want to get the hang of it, think how you would like to become a slug or a crab....

... The Man in Christ rose again: not only the God. That is the whole point. For the first time we saw a real man. One tin soldier—real tin, just like the rest—had come fully and splendidly alive."[4]

II. An Explanation: Two Natures in One Person

The most beautiful and breathtaking nativity scene is found in Philippians 2:5–7.

> Have this attitude in yourselves which was also in Christ Jesus, who, although He existed in the form of God, did not regard equality with God a thing to be grasped, but emptied Himself, taking the form of a bond-servant, and being made in the likeness of men.

In this sacred scene, divine humility glows in the subdued light of the Incarnation, bathed in hues of another world. The Creator willingly submitted to the laws of the very universe He had created. He released independence and became dependent. He gave up being the one served to become the servant.

A. The God-Man as God. In emptying Himself, the Son did not shed His deity; in becoming a man, He did not become something less than God. Rather, He voluntarily released His grasp on His divine prerogatives and set aside the independent use of His powers as deity.

4. C. S. Lewis, *Mere Christianity,* rev. and enl. (1952; reprint, New York, N.Y.: Macmillan Publishing Co., 1960), pp. 139–40.

B. The God-Man as man. As a man, Jesus could do two things He was unable to do as God: be tempted by Satan and die. Hebrews 4:14–16 shows us how this affects our relationship to Him.

> Since then we have a great high priest who has passed through the heavens, Jesus the Son of God, let us hold fast our confession. For we do not have a high priest who cannot sympathize with our weaknesses, but one who has been tempted in all things as we are, yet without sin. Let us therefore draw near with confidence to the throne of grace, that we may receive mercy and may find grace to help in time of need.

We have a Savior who has been there—walked where we walk . . . hurt where we hurt . . . cried where we cry . . . ached where we ache. And so, when we come to Him in time of need, He does not scold us or shake His head in irritated disgust. He is sympathetic. When Jesus was cut, He bled; when He was sad, He wept; when He got hungry, His stomach gnawed within; when He got cold, He shivered; when He got hot, He sweated; when His heart stopped, He died. Because He was a man He can sympathize with our weakness, yet without ever succumbing to sin. He withstood the full fury of temptation—one hundred percent of the agonizing attacks of Satan, the full measure of the tiring and emotionally wrenching ordeal. Because He experienced Satan's attacks to the end without giving in, He endured greater temptation than us—not less.

III. Some Illustrations: Both Natures Revealed Back-to-Back

Numerous eyewitnesses cite instances where deity peeks through the drawn curtain of Jesus' humanity.

A. Matthew 14:22–33. In verses 22–23, Jesus shows His humanity through His dependence on the Father in prayer.

> And immediately He made the disciples get into the boat, and go ahead of Him to the other side, while He sent the multitudes away. And after He had sent the multitudes away, He went up to the mountain by Himself to pray; and when it was evening, He was there alone.

In verses 24–27, He demonstrates His deity by walking on the water.

> But the boat was already many stadia away from the land, battered by the waves; for the wind was contrary. And in the fourth watch of the night He came to them, walking on the sea. And when the disciples

saw Him walking on the sea, they were frightened, saying, "It is a ghost!" And they cried out for fear. But immediately Jesus spoke to them, saying, "Take courage, it is I; do not be afraid."

In the verses that follow, this unveiling of deity resulted in worship and a confession of belief on the part of the disciples.

B. Luke 8:22–25. In a scene similar to the one we saw in Matthew, we see Jesus on the sea again, this time weary and needing rest.

Now it came about on one of those days, that He and His disciples got into a boat, and He said to them, "Let us go over to the other side of the lake." And they launched out. But as they were sailing along He fell asleep; and a fierce gale of wind descended upon the lake, and they began to be swamped and to be in danger. And they came to Him and woke Him up, saying, "Master, Master, we are perishing!" And being aroused, He rebuked the wind and the surging waves, and they stopped, and it became calm. And He said to them, "Where is your faith?" And they were fearful and amazed, saying to one another, "Who then is this, that He commands even the winds and the water, and they obey Him?"

The humanity of Christ can be seen in the deep sleep He had succumbed to, while His deity is clearly shown in His commanding power over the wind and waves.

C. John 11:32–36, 41–46. Jesus had often gone to Bethany to rest and refresh Himself among the family of Mary, Martha, and Lazarus. On this occasion, however, we see the Savior in grief and unrest.

Therefore, when Mary came where Jesus was, she saw Him, and fell at His feet, saying to Him, "Lord, if You had been here, my brother would not have died." When Jesus therefore saw her weeping, and the Jews who came with her, also weeping, He was deeply moved in spirit, and was troubled, and said, "Where have you laid him?" They said to Him, "Lord, come and see." Jesus wept. And so the Jews were saying, "Behold how He loved him!"

In the shortest, but one of the most profoundly penetrating verses of Scripture—"Jesus wept"—the humanity of Jesus pours from the page. At the tomb of Lazarus, a gamut of emotions runs through Jesus: He was "deeply moved" and "was troubled" and finally "wept." But back-to-back with this unguarded display of humanity we see the deity of Christ stand tall and resolute in verses 41–44 when He raises Lazarus from the dead.

And so they removed the stone. And Jesus raised His eyes, and said, "Father, I thank Thee that Thou heardest Me. And I knew that Thou hearest me always; but because of the people standing around I said it, that they may believe that Thou didst send Me." And when He had said these things, He cried out with a loud voice, "Lazarus, come forth." He who had died came forth, bound hand and foot with wrappings; and his face was wrapped around with a cloth. Jesus said to them, "Unbind him, and let him go."

IV. Practical Results: How Both Bring Benefit

The union of deity and humanity in the person of Christ is referred to in theological circles as the hypostatic union. As dry and static as that may sound, this doctrine is not a dusty piece of academic trivia. It is both vibrant and vital to our experience of the Christian life. Because Jesus is God, He is able to authentically forgive sins (Mark 2:7), to understand our deepest needs and weaknesses (Heb. 2:17, 4:15), and to be a mediator between God and man (Gal. 3:20, 1 Tim. 2:5).

The Prince Who Became a Pauper

In the Lerner and Loewe musical *Camelot,* King Arthur is confronted by Queen Guinevere's infidelity with the king's most trusted knight, Lancelot. Under the law, she was judged guilty and sentenced to be burned at the stake. Arthur was caught emotionally between his love for his wife and his responsibility to the law. Mordred, Arthur's illegitimate son, articulated the painful position the king was in:

Arthur! What a magnificent dilemma! Let her die, your life is over; let her live, your life's a fraud. Which will it be, Arthur? Do you kill the Queen or kill the law?[5]

With tears in his eyes, King Arthur moves to the castle window to watch the execution. The executioner is waiting for the signal from the king to light the torch, but Arthur's pain is overpowering.

I can't! I can't! I can't let her die![6]

To which Mordred replies:

Well, you're human after all, aren't you, Arthur? Human and helpless.[7]

---

5. Allan Knee, ed., *Idylls of the King AND Camelot* (New York, N.Y.: Dell Publishing Co., 1967), p. 241.

6. Knee, *Idylls AND Camelot,* p. 241.

7. Knee, *Idylls AND Camelot,* p. 241.

Unlike Arthur, Jesus was not "human and helpless." He was God. Philippians 2 describes the scene of a King—greater than Arthur—who left His kingdom behind, who emptied Himself, taking the form of a man and becoming obedient to the point of death. A King who left the comforts and splendor of the castle to take the place of His Guinevere (2 Cor. 8:9). In doing so, both justice *and* love were satisfied. Picture yourself as Guinevere: guilty, awaiting execution. And then the King comes down to put Himself in your place. To pay the penalty for your sin. How will you respond? Can you do anything but fall before Him and wash His feet with your tears?

 Living Insights

Study One ▬▬▬▬▬▬▬▬▬▬▬▬▬▬▬▬▬▬▬▬▬▬▬▬▬▬▬▬▬▬▬▬

The God-Man as God was free from sin, yet as man he was fully human. This study included a look at both natures as evidenced in the four Gospels. Let's use our Living Insights today to hitchhike on that study style.

● Reproduce this chart in your notebook. As you study these accounts from the four Gospel writers, look for observations that specifically relate to Christ's humanity, and specifically state His deity. You may want to focus on only one or two accounts, or try to do all four. But please, don't be in a hurry.

Humanity Exemplified	Deity Emphasized
Matthew 20:29–34	
Mark 3:1–6	

Chart continued on next page

Humanity Exemplified	Deity Emphasized
Luke 7:11–17	
John 2:1–11	

 Living Insights

Study Two

The best way to deepen your confidence in Christ is to make a personal study of the Scriptures—to focus attention on the person and work of Jesus.

- Let's use our time today to think through our commitment to study the Word of God. Are you committed to doing this? If not, would you consider taking that step now? How can you go about your study? How will you endeavor to be consistent? What tools will be necessary? When is the best time? Think about this . . . jot down thoughts . . . make the appropriate plans with God.

Jesus: A Lamb Led to Slaughter
Isaiah 53, Matthew 26, John 19:17–30

Max Lucado, in his excellent book *No Wonder They Call Him the Savior,* writes of the beauty and grandeur of God's dramatic display of love on the cross.

Nearing the climax of the story, God, motivated by love and directed by divinity, surprised everyone. He became a man. In an untouchable mystery, he disguised himself as a carpenter and lived in a dusty Judean village. Determined to prove his love for his creation, he walked incognito through his own world. His calloused hands touched wounds and his compassionate tongue touched hearts. He became one of us. . . .

But as beautiful as this act of incarnation was, it was not the zenith. Like a master painter God reserved his masterpiece until the end. All the earlier acts of love had been leading to this one. The angels hushed and the heavens paused to witness the finale. God unveils the canvas and the ultimate act of creative compassion is revealed.

God on a cross.

The Creator being sacrificed for the creation. God convincing man once and for all that forgiveness still follows failure.[1]

I. Death: Jesus' Constant Companion

"Born to die" was an epigram that followed Billy the Kid until the time of his violent and early death. Born to die. The phrase has been hung on many a young, hardened criminal. But the cruel shoe fit Christ better than it did any person in history's hall of shame. Every day the shadow of the cross stretched long across His path. Before He was even two, an assassination plot by Herod almost put an end to His tender life (Matt. 2:16). By the time He could read, He learned the Old Testament prophecies of His death (Ps. 22, Isa. 53). At thirty-three, when most men are beginning their careers, He was ending His.

A. His purpose for coming. Before Mary's pregnancy reached full term, the destiny of her baby was determined. The obituary of Isaiah 53 perched like a vulture over the crib of the Christ child. Sorrow, grief, and pain all synchronized their watches for the time when their day would come, when they would have their chance to bully and beat and bruise Him.

He was despised and forsaken of men,
A man of sorrows, and acquainted with grief;
And like one from whom men hide their face,

---

1. Max Lucado, *No Wonder They Call Him the Savior* (Portland, Oreg.: Multnomah Press, 1986), pp. 57–58.

He was despised, and we did not esteem Him.
Surely our griefs He Himself bore,
And our sorrows He carried;
Yet we ourselves esteemed Him stricken,
Smitten of God, and afflicted.
But He was pierced through for our transgressions,
He was crushed for our iniquities;
The chastening for our well-being fell upon Him,
And by His scourging we are healed.
All of us like sheep have gone astray,
Each of us has turned to his own way;
But the Lord has caused the iniquity of us all
To fall on Him.
He was oppressed and He was afflicted,
Yet He did not open His mouth;
Like a lamb that is led to slaughter. (vv. 3–7a)

A lamb led to the slaughter. The tender child would not grow up a doctor . . . or lawyer . . . or rabbi; He would not marry; He would not carry on the family name; He would not even be there to care for His aging mother. He would be a Passover lamb slaughtered as a sacrifice for sin. He would be a baby born to die.

B. His comments during ministry. Not only was the death of Christ prophesied in the Old Testament, but it was foretold by His own lips in several New Testament passages.

  1. Matthew 16:21–23. Following the incident in which Peter acknowledged Jesus to be the Messiah, Jesus began to prepare His disciples for the bitter reality of His imminent suffering and death.

> From that time Jesus Christ began to show His disciples that He must go to Jerusalem, and suffer many things from the elders and chief priests and scribes, and be killed, and be raised up on the third day. And Peter took Him aside and began to rebuke Him, saying, "God forbid it, Lord! This shall never happen to You." But He turned and said to Peter, "Get behind Me, Satan! You are a stumbling block to Me; for you are not setting your mind on God's interests, but man's."

  2. Matthew 17:22–23. Intent on charting the road to the cross, Matthew again chronicled the cryptic words of Jesus.

> And while they were gathering together in Galilee, Jesus said to them, "The Son of Man is going to be delivered into the hands of men; and they will kill Him, and He will be raised on the third day." And they were deeply grieved.

3. **Matthew 20:17–19a.** Like a recurring, resonant note in a funeral dirge, Jesus again struck the somber chord concerning His crucifixion.

> And as Jesus was about to go up to Jerusalem, He took the twelve disciples aside by themselves, and on the way He said to them, "Behold, we are going up to Jerusalem; and the Son of Man will be delivered to the chief priests and scribes, and they will condemn Him to death, and will deliver Him to the Gentiles to mock and scourge and crucify Him."

4. **Matthew 26:1–2.** Two days before the storm of the Crucifixion, Jesus was in Jerusalem in the calm eye of the religious city's Passover preparations. Like a captain standing at the mast and scanning the horizon for signs of a storm, Jesus alerted His sailors—His fishers of men—about the waves that were about to batter their ship.

> And it came about that when Jesus had finished all these words, He said to His disciples, "You know that after two days the Passover is coming, and the Son of Man is to be delivered up for crucifixion."

5. **Matthew 26:6–13.** While Jesus was enjoying an eleventh-hour respite at Simon the leper's house in Bethany, a woman poured perfume on His head as He reclined at the dinner table. The disciples were indignant at the extravagant waste, explaining that it could have been used to help the poor. But Jesus defended her act of devotion and again revealed His imminent fate.

> But Jesus, aware of this, said to them, "Why do you bother the woman? For she has done a good deed to Me. For the poor you have with you always; but you do not always have Me. For when she poured this perfume upon My body, she did it to prepare Me for burial." (vv. 10–12)

C. **His statement to the disciples.** It was night when Christ celebrated the Last Supper with His disciples in the upper room. Several oil lamps dotted the room, sending a gallery of shadows to loiter against the walls, watching. Satan was there, too, waiting to enter into Judas (John 13:27). The brow of Jesus was knitted; His eyes, intense. A hush fell over the room as He spoke: " 'Truly, truly, I say to you, that one of you will betray Me' " (v. 21). The room winced, shadows miming every move. The water was further troubled by Jesus' indicting words to Peter: " 'Truly, truly, I

say to you, a cock shall not crow, until you deny Me three times' "
(v. 38b). The disciples were stunned. Their leader was about to be
betrayed . . . and denied . . . with the betrayal and denial coming
from within the ranks of those who had been closest to Him. It was
no wonder they were deeply troubled. And it was no surprise
—knowing their Savior who had calmed both wind and waves
before—that He would now speak to calm their troubled hearts.

"Let not your heart be troubled; believe in God, believe
also in Me. In My Father's house are many dwelling
places; if it were not so, I would have told you; for I
go to prepare a place for you. And if I go and prepare
a place for you, I will come again, and receive you
to Myself; that where I am, there you may be also."
(14:1–3)

Matthew informs us that the upper room discourse was closed
with a hymn, and after the hymn, they went to the Mount of
Olives to pray and to await the betrayal (Matt. 26:30).

II. Arrest and Trials: The Shadow Lengthens

The hymn seemed to hold the shadow of death at bay, but when it
was over, dark and dreadful thoughts lengthened to overtake the
conversation.

Then Jesus said to them, "You will all fall away because
of Me this night, for it is written, 'I will strike down the
shepherd, and the sheep of the flock shall be scattered.' "
(Matt. 26:31)

Peter again verbalizes his undying loyalty: " 'Even though all may
fall away because of You, I will never fall away' " (v. 33). " 'Even if I
have to die with You, I will not deny You' " (v. 35). The others fervently
echoed Peter's resolve. But it would be the words of Christ that would
stand. The Shepherd would be struck down; the sheep, scattered.

A. In the garden (Matt. 26:36–46). Jesus led the disciples to the
little garden spot known as Gethsemane to pray. He would have
the others sit and wait while He took Peter, James, and John
with Him. Christ stood on the dark precipice overlooking the
valley of death. For the world to have light and life, He would
have to jump into the blackness to be dashed upon the altar of
jagged rocks below. Fear knotted His stomach. The agony was
unbearable.

Then He said to them, "My soul is deeply grieved, to
the point of death; remain here and keep watch with
Me." And He went a little beyond them, and fell on His
face and prayed, saying, "My Father, if it is possible,
let this cup pass from Me; yet not as I will, but as
Thou wilt." (vv. 38–39)

25

The vigilante mob arrived (v. 47). The kiss of Judas sealed the betrayal (vv. 48–49). The Shepherd was taken captive (vv. 50–55). The sheep were scattered (v. 56).

┌─ *The Gift of Gethsemane* ──────────────────────────────
│ Looking through the shadowy foliage of Gethsemane, we
│ don't see the classic portrait of Christ rendered by the
│ artist. We don't see Him in a snow-white robe kneeling
│ beside a big rock, hands peacefully folded, with a look of
│ serenity in His face as a spotlight from heaven illuminates
│ His golden-brown hair. Instead, we see a man flat on His
│ face, fists pounding the hard earth in agony. We see a face
│ stained with tears and dirt, hair matted with sweat, facial
│ muscles contorted in pain like the gnarled, twisted olive
│ trees looking on. God was never more human than at this
│ hour. Have you been in the dark garden of Gethsemane?
│ Betrayed by a friend? Deserted by those around you? Felt
│ abandoned? Lonely? The next time you think no one cares,
│ pay a visit to Gethsemane and see the man of sorrows. Because seeing God like this does wonders for your suffering.
└──

B. Before the authorities. If there was ever a miscarriage of justice, if ever a breach of truth, if ever a blinding of conscience, it happened on this night of infamy when the Creator was brought to trial before His creatures. There were six trials that sleepless night. The first three were conducted by the Jewish authorities and concerned religious questions; the final three concerned civil questions and were conducted by the Roman authorities. In the first trial, Annas, father-in-law of Caiaphas the high priest, examined Jesus (John 18:12–24). In the second trial, Caiaphas and the Sanhedrin quickly condemned Him, found Him guilty of blasphemy, then mocked and beat Him (Matt. 26:57–66). In the third trial, the Sanhedrin "took counsel against Jesus to put Him to death" (27:1–2). Since the Jews could not legally carry out an execution, they turned Christ over to the Roman authorities. Pilate, governor of Judea, presided over this fourth trial (vv. 2, 11–14). But Pilate found Christ innocent (John 18:38). When the wishy-washy leader heard that Jesus had come from Galilee (Luke 23:5), he seized the opportunity to pass the judicial buck to Herod, Galilee's governor, who was also in Jerusalem at the time (v. 7). Herod Antipas was awakened and presided over the trial (vv. 8–12). But Herod, too, found no guilt in Jesus, and tossed the ball back into Pilate's court (vv. 14b–15). In the final trial, Pilate again declared Christ innocent (v. 14), but the incensed crowd outside was in a frenzy for blood. The situation was volatile. Facing a riot, Pilate succumbed to the pressure of the crowd. Washing his hands from the guilt of shedding innocent blood, Pilate gave Jesus over to be crucified (Matt. 27:24–26).

III. The Cross: *Tetelestai* (John 19:17–30)

A sleepless night of indignity. False witnesses slandering . . . beatings . . . thorns placed on the King of King's head . . . a robe and scepter of mock royalty . . . more scourging . . . more mocking. By 9 A.M. His hands and feet were nailed to a rough-cut cross that was lifted up and dropped with a dull thud into Golgotha's brow. From noon to three, darkness fell over the earth—truly the darkest hours in human history. John, the disciple whom Christ loved, was an eyewitness to the Crucifixion. He records for us the final minutes of this tragic scene in chapter 19 of his Gospel.

> After this, Jesus, knowing that all things had already been accomplished, in order that the Scripture might be fulfilled, said, "I am thirsty." A jar full of sour wine was standing there; so they put a sponge full of the sour wine upon a branch of hyssop, and brought it up to His mouth. When Jesus therefore had received the sour wine, He said, "It is finished!" And He bowed His head, and gave up His spirit. (vv. 28–30)

Jesus takes a drink, as if to clear His parched throat so His clarion call could be heard by all: *Tetelestai*—"It is finished!" If the Crucifixion was the darkest moment in history, these words pierced through the clouds like a radiant beam of sunlight. The words don't refer to the completion of His sufferings but the completion of the task He was born to do—to save His people from their sins (Matt. 1:21). It is a cry of victory. With these words, fetters burst, prison walls crumbled, barriers fell, and gates which had been closed for thousands of years began to turn on their rusty hinges. The rough-cut timber of the cross formed the bridge over sin's troubled waters and spanned hell's chasm, uniting earth and heaven. With the words "It is finished," the bridge was complete. It was a cry of victory . . . a cry of accomplishment . . . and yes, a cry of relief. Jesus could now exchange His thorns for a crown, His nakedness for a robe, His disgrace for glory, His wounds for worship.

The Bridge over Troubled Water

If you're without Christ, you're treading water in a sea of sin. Things may appear calm, and you may feel you've got everything under control now. But one day you'll go under and sink like a rock and drown. The only life preserver is Jesus; the only way to heaven is the bridge of the cross. You can't swim to the other side on your own strength. If you're in that situation, you can call out to Jesus—as Peter did when he was sinking—"Lord, save me!" (Matt. 14:30). It doesn't need to be a King James prayer or a Revised Standard confession. It just needs to be from your heart to His. And when these two hearts connect, your bridge to heaven is complete. Isn't it about time you stopped treading and started trusting?

 Living Insights

Study One ▬▬▬▬▬▬▬▬▬▬▬▬▬▬▬▬▬▬▬▬▬▬▬▬▬▬▬▬

We briefly touched on some Old Testament prophecies about Christ by referring to Isaiah 53. Let's look further into the Old Testament predictions concerning the Messiah.

- Copy this chart into your notebook. As you look up these Old Testament passages, jot down the prophecies. If you're really up to a challenge, track down the New Testament passages that fulfill these prophecies.

Old Testament Passage	Messianic Prophecy	New Testament Passage
Genesis 3:15		
Genesis 49:10		
2 Samuel 7:16		
Psalm 2:2		
Psalm 16:10		
Psalm 22:1–18		
Isaiah 7:13–14		
Isaiah 9:6		
Isaiah 61:1		
Daniel 9:25–26		
Hosea 2:23		
Micah 5:2		
Haggai 2:7		
Zechariah 9:9		
Zechariah 11:11–13		
Zechariah 13:7		
Malachi 3:1–2		

Living Insights

For some of us, it is only when we see the specifics about Christ's death that we come to grips with the agony of it all. And then to think that He endured it . . . *for us.*

● There are several ways to properly respond to a study of this nature. Some that come to mind:
—Thank Him
—Trust Him
—Worship Him
—Love Him
—Praise Him
Let's take our time to do some of these right now. You may do them silently, verbally, in writing, in singing . . . in your own way. *O come, let us adore Him.*

God digs the well of joy deep; He digs the well of joy deep with sorrow.

Jesus: Triumphant over the Grave

John 20

It was a morning like any other in the ancient Roman city. Men and women went about their business as usual, working hard in the bright sunlight and resting easy in the cool shade of the mountain. Children romped just as they did yesterday and the day before that, and many worshiped their idols in the pagan temples, eating, drinking, and being merry, living life to the hilt in their normal, reckless way. Yet in a few precious hours, they would all be dead—the fury of Mount Vesuvius would erupt to encase Pompeii in a tomb of lava for centuries to come.

About forty years before Pompeii was destroyed, another eruption had taken place that shook the foundations of heaven and earth. An ordinary woman had come to the tomb of her beloved friend, just as she had probably done the day before and the day before that. But today, she was horrified by an open grave—the body missing; the stone rolled away. She ran away in her terror and grief, but what she didn't know then was that the tomb had erupted with the power of God. The crucified Son of God had risen, triumphantly conquering death and bringing new life to a human race encased in sin since time began.

I. Jesus' Prediction of His Resurrection

Paul reasons in 1 Corinthians 15 that "if Christ has not been raised, your faith is worthless" (v. 17) and "if the dead are not raised, 'let us eat and drink, for tomorrow we die' " (v. 32b). If Jesus did not rise from the dead, Christianity is no better than the pagan religions of Pompeii. But His triumph over the grave gave Christianity a unique distinctive: its founder *lives!* Early in the Gospel accounts, Jesus predicted not only His death—but also His resurrection.

A. A sign requested. In 1 Corinthians 1:22, Paul writes that the "Jews ask for signs, and Greeks search for wisdom." This tendency on the part of the Jews to walk by sight as opposed to faith is illustrated in Matthew 12, where the scribes and Pharisees demanded a sign from Jesus. But He refused to pander to these religious voyeurs, and answered with a barbed rebuke,

> "An evil and adulterous generation craves for a sign; and yet no sign shall be given to it but the sign of Jonah the prophet." (v. 39)

B. "The sign of Jonah." Instead of an immediate, nickel-and-dime show of power, Jesus announces a future sign so spectacular that one would have to be blind to miss it.

> "For just as Jonah was three days and three nights in the belly of the sea monster, so shall the Son of Man

Joe Bailey- who buried three sons
The View from a Hearse 30

be three days and three nights in the heart of the
earth." (v. 40)

Quoting Jonah 1:17, Jesus predicted His resurrection and claimed
that His interment would last no longer than three days and
nights. Just as Jonah emerged alive from the belly of the great
fish, so the bowels of the earth would open to release Jesus.[1]

II. Pertinent Issues Related to Jesus' Resurrection

If we build a bridge from Matthew 12 to John 19, we move directly
from "the sign of Jonah" to the sight of Jesus on Golgotha. In
Matthew 12, we see Him sparkling with life as He clashes with the
Pharisees. In John 19, we see Him lay down His sword at the cross
in a final act of submission.

A. Certainty of His death. Some have sought to explain away
Christ's appearances after His death with something known as
the "swoon theory." This theory says Christ did not die but
merely fainted from the physical and emotional trauma of the
cross, and later revived in the coolness of the tomb. The
evidence, however, conclusively argues against this speculation.
First, the testimony of Scripture clearly states that Jesus died.

When Jesus therefore had received the sour wine, He
said, "It is finished!" And He bowed His head, and
gave up His spirit. (John 19:30)

Second, the actions of the soldiers around the cross corroborate
the claims.[2]

The soldiers therefore came, and broke the legs of
the first man, and of the other man who was crucified
with Him; but coming to Jesus, when they saw that
He was already dead, they did not break His legs.
(vv. 32–33)

Third, the testimony of the physiological data supports the fact
of Christ's death.[3]

But one of the soldiers pierced His side with a spear,
and immediately there came out blood and water.
(v. 34)

Finally, the actions of the burial party indicate the certainty of
Jesus' death (vv. 38–42). Had there been any indication of life,

1. Other passages where Jesus spoke of His resurrection are Matthew 16:21, 17:22–23, 20:18–19;
Mark 10:32–34.

2. The normal cause of death in crucifixion was suffocation. The chest cavity would collapse
under the hanging weight of the body. In order to breathe, the victim would have to push up
with the legs to a more erect position. To hurry death, the legs would be broken, thus
preventing the victim from being able to breathe.

3. When the blood's thicker plasma separates from the thinner serum, it is a sign of certain
death.

those preparing Him for burial would have tried to revive Him. Instead, they embalmed the body and placed it in the tomb.[4]

A Sermon in Suffering

The centurion who was standing in front of Christ when He died exclaimed in awe: "Truly this man was the Son of God!" (Mark 15:39).

If it is true that a picture paints a thousand words, then there was a Roman centurion who got a dictionary full. All he did was see Jesus suffer. He never heard him preach or saw him heal or followed him through the crowds. He never witnessed him still the wind; he only witnessed the way he died. . . .

Maybe that's what moved this old, crusty soldier. Serenity in suffering is a stirring testimony.[5]

B. Material evidence. In John 20:1–7, three important pieces of material evidence support Christ's resurrection: the displaced stone, the empty tomb, and the linen wrappings.

Now on the first day of the week Mary Magdalene came early to the tomb, while it was still dark, and saw the stone already taken away from the tomb. And so she ran and came to Simon Peter, and to the other disciple whom Jesus loved, and said to them, "They have taken away the Lord out of the tomb, and we do not know where they have laid Him." Peter therefore went forth, and the other disciple, and they were going to the tomb. And the two were running together; and the other disciple ran ahead faster than Peter, and came to the tomb first; and stooping and looking in, he saw the linen wrappings lying there; but he did not go in. Simon Peter therefore also came, following him, and entered the tomb; and he beheld the linen wrappings lying there, and the face-cloth, which had been on His head, not lying

---

4. According to the burial customs of that time, a corpse was wrapped tightly with cloth in which aromatic spices were interspersed. This covered the stench of death and formed an adhesive seal around the body. We are told that one hundred pounds of aloes and myrrh were purchased for Christ's burial. The tightly wrapped cloths with the gummy spices formed a mummylike cocoon, as described in the account where Jesus raised Lazarus (John 11:44).

5. Max Lucado, *No Wonder They Call Him the Savior* (Portland, Oreg.: Multnomah Press, 1986), p. 77.

with the linen wrappings, but rolled up in a place by itself.

The burial wrappings, made rigid by the resin from the spices, formed a shell, a type of cocoon, that now lay empty on the cold rock slab in the tomb. Only the face covering, which was a band wound like a turban, was disheveled and rolled up in a place off to one side. The immediate impression of Mary Magdalene was that the body had been stolen (v. 2). Apparently, this was the initial reaction of Peter and John (vv. 8–9). But logically, who would have kidnapped it? Neither the Jews nor the Romans wanted an empty tomb. They wanted Christ dead and buried. If they had stolen it, they would merely have had to produce the body, and the claim of the Resurrection would have been discredited. The guards, whose very lives were at stake in safeguarding the body, wouldn't have dared to steal the body or allow it to be stolen. Finally, the alarm expressed by the disciples precludes them from being suspects. Neither friend nor foe had a logical motive to kidnap the body. Again, the evidence points to a literal, bodily resurrection.

C. **Physical appearances.** The New Testament records no less than eleven physical encounters with the risen Christ. These encounters occurred at different times, in different places, and with a variety of individuals. It has often been argued that these people merely had grief-induced hallucinations. However, Jesus once appeared to more than five hundred people at one time (1 Cor. 15:6). For so many people to have shared the same hallucination at the same time strains the imagination far more than the probability of Christ's bodily resurrection. John, an eyewitness to the death of Christ, records three postresurrection appearances: one with Mary outside the tomb (John 20:11–18), one with the disciples behind closed doors (vv. 19–23), and one with Thomas (vv. 24–29). Christ's appearance to Thomas is awesome and arresting.

> But Thomas, one of the twelve, called Didymus, was not with them when Jesus came. The other disciples therefore were saying to him, "We have seen the Lord!" But he said to them, "Unless I shall see in His hands the imprint of the nails, and put my finger into the place of the nails, and put my hand into His side, I will not believe." And after eight days again His disciples were inside, and Thomas with them. Jesus came, the doors having been shut, and stood in their midst, and said, "Peace be with you." Then He said to Thomas, "Reach here your finger, and see My

hands; and reach here your hand, and put it into My side; and be not unbelieving, but believing." Thomas answered and said to Him, "My Lord and my God!" Jesus said to him, "Because you have seen Me, have you believed? Blessed are they who did not see, and yet believed."

Learning from Thomas

In our unstretched, rigid imaginations, we strain to make room in our thinking for miracles. Like Thomas, we are so used to living by sight rather than by faith that we are constantly looking for hands with nail prints. We are used to working with statistical probabilities and empirical evidence, while God characteristically works with impossibilities and the evidence of things not seen (Luke 1:37, Heb. 11:1). How about you? How supple is your imagination? When is the last time the impossible rearranged the furniture of your thinking? Or sight bowed to faith in your relationship with Christ? Remember Jesus' words to Thomas: " 'Blessed are they who did not see, and yet believed' " (John 20:29).

D. Historical results. At the time of the cross, the disciples had scattered like scared sheep (Matt. 26:56). After seeing the empty tomb, they believed with Mary that someone had stolen the body, and they went away to their own homes (John 20:2, 8–10). There they hid, cowering, shuttered away for fear of the Jews (v. 19). However, after they had seen the risen Christ, this weak-kneed band of deserters turned the world upside down (Acts 17:6). Even Peter, who denied Christ so emphatically, preached boldly about Him in the very city where He was only recently executed (Acts 2:14–36). The descent of the Holy Spirit and the birth of the Church are two other historical ramifications of the Resurrection (Acts 1–2).

III. The Lasting Benefits

Never were the arms of God opened so wide as when they were outstretched on the cross. Like a father embracing his prodigal son, the arms of Jesus reached out to give a wayward world the embrace of forgiveness to all who would come home. May God give you the grace to look at the nail prints in the hands of the risen Savior and fall on your face before Him, as did Thomas, proclaiming through tears: "My Lord and my God!" For the Resurrection not only assures us that Jesus is God, but that we are forgiven and will also be resurrected after our death to live forever in His presence (1 Cor. 15).

Living Insights

Study One ━━━━━━━━━━━━━━━━━━━━━━━━━━━━━━━

The doctrine of the Resurrection is no more clearly described than in 1 Corinthians 15. Having studied the historic account from the Gospels, let's turn our attention to the theological significance.

• Let's do some careful observation of this landmark chapter. Construct the following chart in your notebook. Record your observations under the appropriate headings.

1 Corinthians 15						
Verses	Who?	What?	Where?	When?	Why?	How?

 Living Insights

Study Two ━━━━━━━━━━━━━━━━━━━━━━━━━━━━━━━

Let's follow through on our study of the Resurrection by making some personal and practical applications.

• Based on 1 Corinthians 15, copy the following chart into your notebook and record all the statements you can personalize into applications.

1 Corinthians 15	
Verses	Applications

Jesus: Ascended and Seated in Heaven

Acts 1:1–11, Ephesians 1:18–23, Hebrews

There are times when it would be great to call God—collect! Or to pull God aside to ask a few questions. Or, at least, to write Him a letter. In the book *Children's Letters to God* the authors have compiled an amusing yet insightful scrapbook of thoughts and questions children have posed to God. Here are a few examples.

Dear God,
    Count me in
            Your friend
            Herbie

Dear God,
    I wrote you before do you remember? Well I did what I promised. But you did not send me the horse yet. What about it?
            Lewis

Dear God,
    Do you get your angels to do all the work? Mommy says we are her angels and we have to do everything.
            Love,
            Maria

Dear God,
    When you started the earth and put people there and all the animals and grass and the stars did you get verey tired? I have a lot of other questions too.
            Very truly yours
            Sherman[1]

Questions. Regardless of how foolish or childish they may seem, they're the best way to get specific answers. A few questions this series might have prompted are: Now that Jesus has died and risen from the grave, what is He doing now? Since Jesus was bodily raised from the dead, does He still operate within a body, or is He just a spirit? When He ascended from earth to heaven, did His position change from what it was originally? With these questions, we'll raise our hands to find out about the present ministry of Jesus—since His ascension. And remember, the only foolish question is the unasked one.

---

1. *Children's Letters to God,* comp. Eric Marshall and Stuart Hample (New York, N.Y.: Simon and Schuster, 1966).

I. The Ascension: When Jesus Christ Left Earth

In Acts 1:1–11, we are told that for forty days after His resurrection Jesus remained in contact with His followers. He spoke, ate, slept, encouraged, instructed, and essentially did all that He had done during His three and a half years with them (see Luke 24). But now it's time for Him to depart. Moments before He ascends to heaven, the disciples raise their hands to wave an eager question before their teacher.

> And so when they had come together, they were asking Him, saying, "Lord, is it at this time You are restoring the kingdom to Israel?" (v. 6)

However, Jesus patiently but firmly shushes the disciples.

> He said to them, "It is not for you to know times or epochs which the Father has fixed by His own authority." (v. 7)

In telling them what they don't need to worry about, Jesus redirects their attention to the page of God's plan that was soon to be turned.

> "But you shall receive power when the Holy Spirit has come upon you; and you shall be My witnesses both in Jerusalem, and in all Judea and Samaria, and even to the remotest part of the earth." (v. 8)

With the promise of the Holy Spirit's presence and power—Jesus speaks His last words on earth and ascends into heaven. Like a rocket slowly lifting off the launchpad, Jesus ascends into the clouds, leaving the awestruck disciples craning their necks, squinting for one last look as He disappears into the sky.

A. Historical fact. The Ascension was public, gradual, and literal; therefore, it could be seen by all.

> And after He had said these things, He was lifted up while they were looking on, and a cloud received Him out of their sight. (v. 9)

B. Practical value. At first glance the doctrine of the Ascension seems like the clouds into which Christ ascended—distant and nebulous. However, understanding the Ascension helps us in at least four ways. First, it helps us appreciate the credibility of Christ. He said He would have to leave the disciples one day (John 14:1–6), and since they actually saw Him leave, the credibility of Christ's word is underscored once more in our thinking. Second, if Christ had not ascended, the Spirit would not have been given to us.

> "But I tell you the truth, it is to your advantage that I go away; for if I do not go away, the Helper shall not come to you; but if I go, I will send Him to you." (16:7)

Third, without His ascension, we would never have received our spiritual gifts.

But to each one of us grace was given according to
the measure of Christ's gift. Therefore it says,
"When He ascended on high,
He led captive a host of captives,
And He gave gifts to men." (Eph. 4:7–8)
Fourth, in Jesus' literal, bodily ascension we have a historic
reminder that His return will also be a literal, bodily return.
"This Jesus, who has been taken up from you into
heaven, will come in just the same way as you have
watched Him go into heaven." (Acts 1:11)

II. Entrance: When Jesus Christ Returned to Heaven

Moving from Acts 1 to Ephesians 1, we leave earth and glimpse the
heavenly side of the Ascension, where the Father has raised Christ
from the dead,
and seated Him at His right hand in the heavenly places,
far above all rule and authority and power and dominion,
and every name that is named, not only in this age, but
also in the one to come. And He put all things in subjection under His feet, and gave Him as head over all things
to the church, which is His body, the fulness of Him who
fills all in all. (Eph. 1:20b–23)
The Father's act of receiving His Son into heaven was His expression
of final approval for Christ's redemptive mission. It was in direct con-
trast to the crown of thorns, scepter, and robe the world gave to Jesus
in mockery. The Father, in a royal coronation ceremony, placed the
King of Kings on His rightful throne "far above all rule and authority
and power and dominion." And in putting "all things in subjection
under His feet," the Father not only gave Jesus dominion over His
enemies (Pss. 2, 110) but over the Church as well (Col. 1:17–20).

Thy Kingdom Come

The kingdom of God is a future era on earth when Jesus will
return to rule His creation. In the meantime, Jesus rules from
heaven. His preceptive will in heaven is done on earth to the
extent that we have enthroned Him in our lives as King
(Matt. 6:9–13). You may have received Jesus years ago as Savior,
but have you enthroned Him as Lord? Are all things in your life
put in subjection under His feet? Don't mock Him in a false display by putting a robe on His shoulders and a scepter in His
hands, pretending, as the Roman soldiers did, to honor Him.
Maybe an ascension needs to take place in your life. Enthrone
Him, won't you? For He is not only the rightful King, but the
worthy King. Worthy to be exalted, honored, obeyed, and most
of all—worthy to be loved.

III. Seated: When Jesus Was Enthroned

Although Christ's earthly mission of redemption is complete—"having offered one sacrifice for sins for all time" (Heb. 10:12)—His heavenly ministry demonstrates that His involvement with man is continuing. The writer to the Hebrews informs us that Jesus is presently our high priest and mediator, our Lord and master, and our companion and friend.

A. **Our high priest and mediator.** We have a great high priest— Jesus, the God-Man—who, though sinless, is sympathetic.

> Since then we have a great high priest who has passed through the heavens, Jesus the Son of God, let us hold fast our confession. For we do not have a high priest who cannot sympathize with our weaknesses, but one who has been tempted in all things as we are, yet without sin. Let us therefore draw near with confidence to the throne of grace, that we may receive mercy and may find grace to help in time of need. (4:14–16)

And because Jesus' priesthood is also permanent, He will eternally defend us before God from Satan's accusations and constantly intercede to forgive our sin and guilt (see Rom. 8:34).

B. **Our sovereign Lord and master.** Jesus not only ministers as our great high priest but as our sovereign Lord and master as well.

> But of the Son He says, . . .
> "Thou hast made him for a little while lower
>   than the angels;
> Thou hast crowned him with glory and
>   honor,
> And hast appointed him over the works of
>   Thy hands;
> Thou hast put all things in subjection
>   under his feet." (2:7–8)

Jesus is intimately involved with mankind by sovereignly calling out a people for Himself, sovereignly functioning as the head of the Church, and sovereignly directing the affairs of life.

C. **Our constant companion and friend.** Because Jesus was God in the flesh and related to man in an eyeball-to-eyeball friendship (see John 11:1–44), we are assured that the distance of His heavenly throne won't separate us from His presence. Repeatedly, the writer to the Hebrews exalts the deity and majesty of the enthroned Savior. Yet, he is careful to underscore that this great high priest, this almighty and sovereign Lord, is also a close companion and friend. He is not ashamed to count us as His most intimate relations.

For both He who sanctifies and those who are sanctified are all from one Father; for which reason He is not ashamed to call them brethren. (2:11)
And like a good friend, He encourages us.

In the same way God, desiring even more to show to the heirs of the promise the unchangeableness of His purpose, interposed with an oath, in order that by two unchangeable things, in which it is impossible for God to lie, we may have strong encouragement, we who have fled for refuge in laying hold of the hope set before us. (6:17–18)

A friend isn't capricious in the relationship, isn't on-again, off-again, isn't fickle. A friend is someone you can count on. And what a friend we have in Jesus—"the same yesterday and today, yes and forever" (Heb. 13:8).

Ashamed of Jesus?

What a beautiful testimony to the humility of Christ that He is not ashamed of us. Think of it! The God of all creation, the great high priest, the sovereign King—not ashamed to have us in His family, not ashamed to call us brothers. Us! When you think about it, it's staggering. But what is even more staggering, more unbelievable, is that we might somehow, in some way, or in some set of circumstances be ashamed of Him.

> Jesus! and shall it ever be,
> A mortal man ashamed of Thee?
> Ashamed of Thee, whom angels praise,
> Whose glories shine through endless days?
>
> Ashamed of Jesus? Sooner far
> Let evening blush to own a star.
> He sheds the beams of light divine
> O'er this benighted soul of mine.
>
> Ashamed of Jesus? Just as soon
> Let midnight be ashamed of noon.
> 'Tis midnight with my soul till He,
> Bright Morning Star, bids darkness flee.
>
> Ashamed of Jesus, that dear Friend
> On whom my hopes of heav'n depend?
> No; when I blush, be this my shame,
> That I no more revere His name.

Ashamed of Jesus? Yes, I may
When I've no guilt to wash away,
No tear to wipe, no good to crave,
No fear to quell, no soul to save.

Till then—nor is my boasting vain—
Till then I boast a Savior slain;
And oh, may this my glory be,
That Christ is not ashamed of me![2]

 Living Insights

Study One ▬▬▬▬▬▬▬▬▬▬▬▬▬▬▬▬▬▬▬▬▬▬▬▬▬▬▬▬

Now that Jesus Christ is seated at the right hand of the Father, what is He doing? This study has allowed us to briefly delve into that question. Copy the following charts into your notebook and spend some time researching the answer from the Word of God, specifically from the book of Hebrews.

- *Christ is our high priest and mediator.* What do "high priest" and "mediator" really mean? Use the following verses to write a clear, concise explanation.

Verses	Clarifications
Heb. 4:14–16	
Heb. 7:23–24	

- *Christ is our sovereign Lord and master.* How do you define "sovereign Lord" and "master"? Use the following verses as a guide to their meanings.

Verses	Clarifications
Heb. 1:8–9	
Heb. 2:7–8	

Continued on next page

2. "Jesus! and Shall It Ever Be," *The Lutheran Hymnal* (Saint Louis, Mo.: Concordia Publishing House, 1941), no. 346.

- *Christ is our constant companion and friend.* Can you explain "constant companion" and "friend"? These verses will be of help in your definitions.

Verses	Clarifications
Heb. 2:11	
Heb. 5:1–2	
Heb. 6:17–18	
Heb. 13:8	

 Living Insights

Study Two ▬▬▬▬▬▬▬▬▬▬▬▬▬▬▬▬▬▬▬▬▬▬▬▬▬▬▬▬▬▬

This study also taught us that Christ's present ministry is vitally important in our lives today and is not there for mere theological study.

- *Christ is our high priest and mediator.* List some areas in your life where you see the application of Christ's priesthood and His role as mediator. Try to use recent examples.
- *Christ is our sovereign Lord and master.* List areas you've surrendered to Christ and then list areas yet unsurrendered. Analyze the contrasts in your life. What is it that keeps you from turning over those areas?
- *Christ is our constant companion and friend.* Jot down some recent illustrations from your life that describe your friendship with Christ. Spend some time talking to your Friend.

Jesus: His Promised Return
Matthew 24, 1 Thessalonians 4:13–18, 2 Peter 3:10–18

It was the war-torn Pacific, March 11, 1942. Sixty-two-year-old General Douglas MacArthur and his family secretly slipped away from the Philippines, and, in a minor miracle, made their way to Australia.

Before General MacArthur left, however, he resolutely promised, "I shall return."[1] More than two and a half years later, on October 20, 1944, he stood again on the soil of the Philippines and announced triumphantly, "I have returned. By the grace of Almighty God, our forces stand again on Philippine soil."[2]

If a man can have that type of resolve and credibility, how much more the Son of God?

Of course, the real question is not whether Jesus will return, or even when, but whether we will be ready to face Him when He does. Doctrinally, most of us believe Jesus will return. However, most have never been emotionally affected by this doctrine.

Scripture tells us that the whole of creation eagerly awaits and anxiously longs for the Savior's return—standing on tiptoes, squinting its eyes, heart aching for when He will come to renew and restore the cosmos.

Can that be said of you? Is the return of Christ simply a tenet of the faith you give an assenting nod to? Or do you *eagerly await* His return—as the Filipinos did MacArthur, or as the New Testament church did Jesus (1 Cor. 1:7, Phil. 3:20)?

I. Christ's Own Predictions of His Return
One possible reason for the lack of *emotional* commitment to Christ's return is the fact that many of us are not *intellectually* convinced of it. The Scriptures, however, are abrim with enough references to convince the most skeptical of Thomases.

A. Several Scriptures. As the disciples watched Jesus ascend, two unidentified men in white clothing stood beside them and said:

> "Men of Galilee, why do you stand looking into the sky? This Jesus, who has been taken up from you into heaven, will come in just the same way as you have watched Him go into heaven." (Acts 1:11)

The promise in Acts 1 is not a new revelation but merely an echo of Christ's earlier words to His disciples in John 14:1–3.

1. *Bartlett's Familiar Quotations,* 14th ed., rev. and enl., ed. Emily Morison Beck (Boston, Mass.: Little, Brown and Company, 1968), p. 959.

2. *Bartlett's,* p. 959.

Describing the terrible drama of the Tribulation, Jesus climactically unfolded His grand entrance, in which He will heroically rescue His imperiled children.

> "But in those days, after that tribulation, the sun will be darkened, and the moon will not give its light, and the stars will be falling from heaven, and the powers that are in the heavens will be shaken. And then they will see the Son of Man coming in clouds with great power and glory. And then He will send forth the angels, and will gather together His elect from the four winds, from the farthest end of the earth, to the farthest end of heaven." (Mark 13:24–27)

Jesus' words, echoed by the two messengers in Acts 1, resolutely proclaim, "I *will* return."

B. General characteristics. Jesus informs us in Mark 13:31–32 that although His coming is certain (v. 31), no one—not the angels, not even He Himself—knows the time of His return; only the Father. However, the Lord has provided certain unmistakable indicators to announce the imminency of His return. Just as emerging buds on winter's brittle branches harbinger spring, so certain signals will herald the return of Christ (vv. 28–29). In Matthew 24, a question arises as to the nature of these burgeoning signs.

> And as He was sitting on the Mount of Olives, the disciples came to Him privately, saying, "Tell us, when will these things be, and what will be the sign of Your coming, and of the end of the age?" (v. 3)

With private candor, Jesus warns that religious deception will mark the beginning of the end times.

> And Jesus answered and said to them, "See to it that no one misleads you. For many will come in My name, saying, 'I am the Christ,' and will mislead many." (vv. 4–5)

Other nubs on the branch will be political unrest along with agricultural and geophysical upheaval.

> "And you will be hearing of wars and rumors of wars; see that you are not frightened, for those things must take place, but that is not yet the end. For nation will rise against nation, and kingdom against kingdom, and in various places there will be famines and earthquakes. But all these things are merely the beginning of birth pangs." (vv. 6–8)

Certainly these signs have existed since the dawn of time, but it is the frequency and intensity of the signs that will toll the twilight knell on earthly history. To alert us to the start of this final age, Christ uses the metaphor of childbirth. Like " 'the beginning of birth pangs,' " wars will become more frequent, more intense. The earth will be a woman in labor, writhing in pain and agony. Turning to a physician's account of this process, we find that Luke charts the patient's progress with even more meticulous detail.

> "And there will be great earthquakes, and in various
> places plagues and famines; and there will be terrors
> and great signs from heaven." (21:11)

Plagues and astronomical phenomena will punctuate the final sentence of earth's history before the Lord's return. Prior to this, however, worldwide persecution of Christians will form a parenthetical paragraph of infamy, inked in the blood of the saints.

> "But before all these things, they will lay their hands
> on you and will persecute you, delivering you to the
> synagogues and prisons, bringing you before kings
> and governors for My name's sake. It will lead to an
> opportunity for your testimony. So make up your
> minds not to prepare beforehand to defend your-
> selves; for I will give you utterance and wisdom which
> none of your opponents will be able to resist or refute.
> But you will be delivered up even by parents and
> brothers and relatives and friends, and they will put
> some of you to death." (vv. 12–16)

Disaster Relief

From South America to Soviet Russia, wars and rumors of wars abound. From Mount Saint Helens to Mexico City, natural disasters rock the world. From Africa to AIDS, brushfires of famine and plague rage out of control. Meanwhile, the population bomb continues to tick, hands upright, pointing to the eleventh hour of planet Earth. But in the midst of that anxious and dramatic hour, Jesus offers us the reassurance of His return.

> "Let not your heart be troubled; believe in God,
> believe also in Me. In My Father's house are
> many dwelling places; if it were not so, I would
> have told you; for I go to prepare a place for
> you. And if I go and prepare a place for you, I
> will come again, and receive you to Myself; that
> where I am, there you may be also." (John 14:1–3)

When He returns, will He receive you? Can you honestly say you have that assurance? Not hope, not wish, but *assurance?* You can be assured He will receive you if first *you* have received Him, for "as many as received Him, to them He gave the right to become children of God, even to those who believe in His name" (1:12).

II. The Distinction between the Rapture and the Second Advent

However black the clouds loom on the horizon of the end times, a silver lining to their edges is formed by the radiant Son who shines behind them. Waiting in the clouds (1 Thess. 4:17), Jesus has arranged an airlift—an emergency evacuation—to deliver His children from the terrors of this Tribulation.[3]

A. "Operation Airlift"—saints removed. Of all the mysterious scenes to occur in the sky, none will be so startling and strange as the Rapture of the Church. Paul hints at this mystery in 1 Corinthians 15:51–53.

> Behold, I tell you a mystery; we shall not all sleep, but we shall all be changed, in a moment, in the twinkling of an eye, at the last trumpet; for the trumpet will sound, and the dead will be raised imperishable, and we shall be changed. For this perishable must put on the imperishable, and this mortal must put on immortality.

The veil to this mystery is further lifted in 1 Thessalonians 4:13–18.

> But we do not want you to be uninformed, brethren, about those who are asleep, that you may not grieve, as do the rest who have no hope. For if we believe that Jesus died and rose again, even so God will bring with Him those who have fallen asleep in Jesus. For this we say to you by the word of the Lord, that we who are alive, and remain until the coming of the Lord, shall not precede those who have fallen asleep. For the Lord Himself will descend from heaven with a shout, with the voice of the archangel, and with the trumpet of God; and the dead in Christ shall rise first. Then we who are alive and remain shall be caught up together with them in the clouds to meet the Lord in the air, and thus we shall always be with the Lord. Therefore comfort one another with these words.

---

3. For more detailed information on the Tribulation, see Revelation 6–19. For an in-depth study, consult *Things to Come* by J. Dwight Pentecost (Findlay, Ohio: Dunham Publishing Company, 1959), pp. 229–369.

B. The judgment seat of Christ—saints rewarded. After we are taken into His arms, we will be ushered before His throne and rewarded for the life we have lived on earth. Here, the true scales of justice will weigh the substance of our deeds, and Jesus Himself will assay the purity of our hearts.

> For we must all appear before the judgment seat of Christ, that each one may be recompensed for his deeds in the body, according to what he has done, whether good or bad. (2 Cor. 5:10)[4]

C. Jesus' return to earth—saints reigning. At the climax of the war of wars, Armageddon, the King of Kings will return to earth to establish His rightful throne. With Him will be all the rewarded believers who will assume roles of responsibility and rule with Him in His kingdom. This millennial reign of Christ will be a golden age of peace and prosperity on the earth (Rev. 19–20), ushered in by His Second Advent.

How Shall We Then Live?

Peter poses a penetrating question as we consider the end times and the promise of Jesus' return: "Since all these things are to be destroyed in this way, what sort of people ought you to be?" (2 Pet. 3:11). Are we to be prophecy freaks, fanatically walking the streets with placards reading "The End Is Near"? Are we to sell all our material belongings and wait on a hillside for the Lord's coming? Or should we play the epicurean tune and "eat, drink, and be merry," divorcing ourselves from world events out of our control? No, Peter urges none of these extremes. Rather, his counsel is sane and sensible.

> But according to His promise we are looking for new heavens and a new earth, in which righteousness dwells. Therefore, beloved, since you look for these things, be diligent to be found by Him in peace, spotless and blameless. (3:13–14)

Not panicked lives, but peaceful. Not polluted lifestyles, but pure.

Continued on next page

4. See also Romans 14:10–12 and 1 Corinthians 3:10–15.

Living Insights

Study One ━━

In our efforts to be balanced, we need to look at Christ's *future* ministry, as well as His past and present ones. Thus, a study of Christ's return is in order.

• The book of Revelation offers the greatest detail of the prophetic future. Copy the following chart into your notebook, and read Revelation 6–19 slowly and deliberately. Whenever something of prophetic significance strikes you, jot it down on your chart.

Revelation 6–19	
Verses	Prophetic Points

 Living Insights

Study Two ━━

The prophetic message not only comforts us about our future, but also asks for a response in our daily lives. Let's look at the practical value of prophecy.

• Our study concluded with a brief look at 2 Peter 3. Let's dig into this chapter a little further, paying particular attention to verses 10–18. After you copy the following chart into your notebook, read the passage carefully and write out what you should be doing and how you should be living in view of prophecy.

2 Peter 3:10–18	
Verses	Practical Points

Jesus: He Is Lord
Ephesians 4

Paul's prayer for the Ephesians was "that Christ may dwell in your hearts" (3:17a, compare John 14:23). When we receive Jesus as Savior, we open the doors of our hearts and let Jesus enter to dine and reside (Rev. 3:20).

However, committing to Him as *Lord* is like transferring the title of our hearts to Him. He comes not only to dine, but also to redesign our lives; not only to reside, but also to renovate.

He goes through every room—not simply to spring-clean our hearts with Windexed works and Pinesoled platitudes but to completely remodel them from ceiling to cellar. With the meticulous precision of an architect, He takes out a door here, puts in a window there; erects a wall where there was permissiveness, and takes out a dark closet where pet sins were once privately fed and nurtured. He rewires our thinking, replumbs our emotions, and expands the square footage of our hearts to dimensions we never dreamed were possible.

What was once a hovel, He transforms into a home—an *Architectural Digest* delight!

I. Jesus: Lord of All My Externals

As Lord, His decisions touch not only what goes on inside, but also what happens on the outside. He is Lord of our relationships, our work, our circumstances, and our bodies—where the rubber of faith meets the road of real life.

A. Lord of my relationships. Paul's prayer in Ephesians 4 reveals a lot about relationships.

> I, therefore, the prisoner of the Lord, entreat you to walk in a manner worthy of the calling with which you have been called, with all humility and gentleness, with patience, showing forbearance to one another in love, being diligent to preserve the unity of the Spirit in the bond of peace. (vv. 1–3)

Is Jesus Lord of your relationships? Does *humility* regulate them? Look at the example of Christ and see if your attitude parallels His.

> Do nothing from selfishness or empty conceit, but with humility of mind let each of you regard one another as more important than himself; do not merely look out for your own personal interests, but also for the interests of others. Have this attitude in yourselves which was also in Christ Jesus, who, although He existed in the form of God, did not regard

equality with God a thing to be grasped, but emptied Himself, taking the form of a bond-servant, and being made in the likeness of men. (Phil. 2:3–7)

The next quality on Paul's list is *gentleness.* Are you gentle to others? The book of Proverbs teaches that "a gentle answer turns away wrath" (15:1a). How do you respond to your children? To your employer or employees? To your neighbor? We have only to put our ear to the door of Mary and Martha's home to hear the gentle words of Christ calm a potentially volatile situation.

But Martha was distracted with all her preparations; and she came up to Him, and said, "Lord, do You not care that my sister has left me to do all the serving alone? Then tell her to help me." But the Lord answered and said to her, "Martha, Martha, you are worried and bothered about so many things; but only a few things are necessary, really only one, for Mary has chosen the good part, which shall not be taken away from her." (Luke 10:40–42)

Patience, forbearance, love, diligence, unity, peace . . . Paul's list goes on. If your relationships have Jesus as Lord, then they should have these qualities. If they don't, there's a big room that you've locked Him out of.

B. Lord of my work. Is there a dichotomy between what goes on in your life on Sunday and what goes on during the rest of the week? Is Jesus Lord of your work as well as your Sabbath?

There is one body and one Spirit, just as also you were called in one hope of your calling; . . . And He gave some as apostles, and some as prophets, and some as evangelists, and some as pastors and teachers. (Eph. 4:4, 11)

A vocation is literally a calling. Often, God calls us into certain fields of service by giving us specific gifts. Just as He gifted some to be apostles, so He gifted others to be artists. As some to be prophets, so others to be physicians. Some, evangelists; others, electricians. Some, pastors and teachers; others, postal workers and therapists. If He's not Lord Monday through Saturday, there's little good in making Him King for a day on Sunday, is there?

C. Lord of my circumstances. Ephesians 4:14–15 reveals another external that the Lord should control—your attitude toward your circumstances.

As a result, we are no longer to be children, tossed here and there by waves, and carried about by every wind of doctrine, by the trickery of men, by craftiness in deceitful scheming; but speaking the truth in love, we are to grow up in all aspects into Him, who is the head, even Christ.

Tossed about by waves? Up one moment, down another? Dry one second, drenched the next? That's the way a child is. Always *under* the circumstances—like a puppet on a string—never on top of them. If Jesus is Lord of your circumstances, all your seas may not be calm—but *you* will be. For you know that He who rules the wind and the waves also rules your circumstances.

D. Lord of my body. The Church is the Body of Christ. When all the members grow up and leave their childish habits and pettiness behind, the body matures and develops, functioning like a well-oiled machine.

> From whom the whole body, being fitted and held together by that which every joint supplies, according to the proper working of each individual part, causes the growth of the body for the building up of itself in love. (v. 16)

However, God's concern for the body doesn't stop with the Church—the spiritual body; it extends to our physical bodies as well. After all, if our bodies are the temple of the Holy Spirit, shouldn't He be concerned if the temple is about to cave in or be condemned (1 Cor. 3:16–17, 2 Cor. 6:14–18)? How about that temple? Is the kitchen your house of worship? Is the refrigerator the cubical Buddha that satisfies all your inner cravings? Or how about the bedroom? Is your bed the altar upon which your morality and integrity are sacrificed? From fattening foods to stolen sex, the body can be a traitor when Jesus isn't enthroned in your life. If the Holy Spirit resides in you, don't you want Him to live in a temple of marble rather than of mud and mire? If so, then your body is what has to go on the altar.

> I urge you therefore, brethren, by the mercies of God, to present your bodies a living and holy sacrifice, acceptable to God, which is your spiritual service of worship. And do not be conformed to this world, but be transformed by the renewing of your mind, that you may prove what the will of God is, that which is good and acceptable and perfect. (Rom. 12:1–2)

II. Jesus: Lord of All My Internals

Getting a grip on the externals is sometimes slippery business—like a three-year-old trying to take hold of a bar of soap in the bathtub. Oddly enough, though, three-year-olds do manage to corral a bar of Ivory now and again. The key to *consistently* managing this elusive task, however, simply comes with maturity. When we grow older, soap is so much easier to handle. The same is true in coming to grips with the lordship of Jesus over the external things in our lives. As we mature internally, we seem to grasp the externals rather naturally. So the real key to having Jesus as master of your externals is to first enthrone Him over your internals—your mind, emotions, and will.

A. Lord of my mind. In the second half of Ephesians 4, Paul stresses the importance of Jesus being Lord of the mind.

> This I say therefore, and affirm together with the Lord, that you walk no longer just as the Gentiles also walk, in the futility of their mind, being darkened in their understanding, excluded from the life of God, because of the ignorance that is in them, because of the hardness of their heart; and they, having become callous, have given themselves over to sensuality, for the practice of every kind of impurity with greediness. (vv. 17–19)

Notice the harsh terms Paul uses to describe a sinful heart: futile, darkened, excluded, ignorant, hard, calloused, *given over* to sensuality, *practicing* every form of impurity, greedy. Hardly the type of heart Christ would feel at home in.

> But you did not learn Christ in this way, if indeed you have heard Him and have been taught in Him, just as truth is in Jesus, that, in reference to your former manner of life, you lay aside the old self, which is being corrupted in accordance with the lusts of deceit, and that you be renewed in the spirit of your mind, and put on the new self, which in the likeness of God has been created in righteousness and holiness of the truth. (vv. 20–24)

Like a filthy shirt reeking with sweat, stained with blood, and saturated with grime, our old selves are to be laid aside and dropped into the trash. And with a renewed mind that is showered and clean, we are to put on the fresh, pure garments of the new self.

B. Lord of my emotions. In verses 25–29, Paul specifically tells how the decision to lay aside the old self and put on the new affects every area of our lives—including our emotions.

> Therefore, laying aside falsehood, speak truth, each one of you, with his neighbor, for we are members of one another. Be angry, and yet do not sin; do not let the sun go down on your anger, and do not give the devil an opportunity. Let him who steals steal no longer; but rather let him labor, performing with his own hands what is good, in order that he may have

something to share with him who has need. Let no unwholesome word proceed from your mouth, but only such a word as is good for edification according to the need of the moment, that it may give grace to those who hear.

If we're not careful, our emotions can take us hostage. Notice the four terrorists Paul unmasks: falsehood (v. 25), anger (v. 26), theft (v. 28), and unwholesome speech (v. 29). Each is ruthless and without scruples. Each, a killer, able to assassinate our character and torch our testimony. Our emotions say "It's OK to lie," or "I have a right to be angry," or "I've got it coming to me," or "So-and-so *needed* telling off." But if Jesus is Lord of our emotions, these victimizing feelings should be met with swift and certain justice. I must tell the truth, even when I feel that it's in my best interest to lie. I must control my temper, even when I feel enraged or wronged. I must work hard to provide for myself and others, even when the easy but dishonest buck entices me. I must muzzle my mouth when it comes to filthy or defamatory talk, and I must train my tongue to lick wounds, not inflict them, even when I've been bitten first.

C. Lord of my will. In verses 30–32, Paul calls on our will to take decisive action.

And do not grieve the Holy Spirit of God, by whom you were sealed for the day of redemption. Let all bitterness and wrath and anger and clamor and slander be put away from you, along with all malice. And be kind to one another, tender-hearted, forgiving each other, just as God in Christ also has forgiven you.

In verse 30, the construction of the Greek verb helps make a dramatic point: "Stop it! Stop grieving the Holy Spirit!" Here, Paul brings us to the crossroads of decision. Are you for Christ or against Him? Whose side are you really on? There's no middle road. No fence to straddle. Ultimately, the whole lordship question boils down to a decision of the will. Are you going to lay aside the old self and enthrone Jesus as Lord—or are you going to continue to walk around in filthy, smelly rags?

My Heart—Christ's Home

Robert Munger's excellent booklet *My Heart—Christ's Home* takes us on a creative but convicting tour of a man's heart, which is described using the imagery of a home. He takes Christ, who has come into his heart, on a brief and self-conscious walk-through. He takes Jesus through the study, where the mind resides; into the dining room, where

---

the appetites and desires dine; into the living room, where his relationship to Christ was vowed to be cultivated; into the workroom, where his talents and skills find their outlet; into the recreation room, where certain questionable associations and activities are entertained; into the bedroom, where the issue of sex rests. Room by room, Jesus beautifully transforms the home. But one day, Jesus notices a stench coming from the hall closet. Some rotting remnant of the man's old life was hidden there—something he was ashamed of, but something he held on to that he didn't want to part with. Do you have a closet like that? As shameful as it may be, let Jesus in to clean it up. Let His sunshine and spring air breeze away the smell. And give the King a castle that is worthy of His presence.

 Living Insights

Study One

We've seen Jesus Christ in the past, present, and future. Now let's look at Jesus Christ *in our own lives.* This study broke down the areas of our lives into four externals and three internals. Spend a few minutes delving into each area. Write down a sentence or two in your notebook that best describes the degree to which you've turned these areas over to Christ.

- My Relationships
- My Work
- My Circumstances
- My Body
- My Mind
- My Emotions
- My Will

 Living Insights

Study Two

Let's use our time today to review and reflect on what we've learned. We hope this brief study about Jesus has produced some new knowledge and has encouraged you to make some changes in your life.

- Copy the following chart into your notebook. As you reflect on these studies, which doctrine stands out the most for you? Which practical thoughts have affected you the most? End by thanking the Lord for what He's done in your life recently.

Jesus, Our Lord		
Lesson Titles	Doctrinal Reflections	Practical Thoughts
Jesus: His Existence Before Creation		
Jesus: A Birth Like None Other		
Jesus: His God-Man Lifestyle		
Jesus: A Lamb Led to Slaughter		
Jesus: Triumphant over the Grave		
Jesus: Ascended and Seated in Heaven		
Jesus: His Promised Return		
Jesus: He Is Lord		

Books for Probing Further

Following Jesus as Lord is like a child following his father's footsteps through the heavy snow. The child is not left to brave the snowstorm alone. But neither does the father spare the child the cold journey—fighting the elements himself while the child warms his hands by the fireplace at home. Rather, the two go through the snow together. As the father leads, the child sees the example and follows the deep footprints that chart a path through the drifts—one step at a time.

Following Jesus as Lord doesn't melt the snow. It doesn't mean instant spring, with sunshine and flowers. The snow will be just as cold; the drifts, just as deep; the blizzards, just as blinding.

But one important thing does change. Where there was a pathless blanket of freezing snow, there now are footprints pressed deep in the drifts before us—and a warm hand outstretched to keep us from slipping.

I hope these studies have encouraged you to take that first step of making Jesus not only your Savior but also your Lord.

The following books should help you along that journey, training your eyes to look not at the deep drifts of snow but at the deep footprints of Christ. And they should also help you to follow Him—one step at a time.

Anderson, Norman. *Jesus Christ: The Witness of History.* Downers Grove, Ill.: InterVarsity Press, 1985. Former director of Advanced Legal Studies at the University of London, the author examines the historical evidences of Christ's life with all the rigorous logic and proofs you would expect from a tenacious trial lawyer.

Bruce, F. F. *Jesus: Lord and Savior.* Downers Grove, Ill.: InterVarsity Press, 1986. In fascinating detail, this noted New Testament scholar examines the biblical evidence that answers the question, Who is Jesus? Doing so, he considers Jesus from His preexistence to His Second Coming.

Green, Michael. *The Empty Cross of Jesus.* Downers Grove, Ill.: InterVarsity Press, 1984. This excellent book examines why Jesus had to die and answers commonly raised objections concerning the Crucifixion and Resurrection.

Griffiths, Michael. *The Example of Jesus.* Downers Grove, Ill.: InterVarsity Press, 1985. Like metal to a magnet, people were drawn to Jesus. Naturally, those who came to know Him wanted to follow His example. The author probes to find out why—and how we, too, can follow the example of Christ.

Lewis, C. S. *Mere Christianity.* Revised and enlarged. 1952. Reprint. New York, N.Y.: Macmillan Publishing Co., 1960. A classic philosophical treatise on the basics of faith in Christ, this helpful book is filled with vivid examples, irrefutable logic, and crackling wit.

Lucado, Max. *No Wonder They Call Him the Savior.* Portland, Oreg.: Multnomah Press, 1986. A book of rare insight, this collection of devotional vignettes plumbs the emotional depths of the cross. You will never look at the Savior's agony quite the same after having been touched by this tender book.

Munger, Robert Boyd. *My Heart—Christ's Home.* Downers Grove, Ill.: InterVarsity Press, 1986. This best-selling booklet examines the lordship of Christ in an extended metaphor—seeing our hearts as homes for Jesus to dwell in and redesign.

Pentecost, J. Dwight. *The Words and Works of Jesus Christ.* Grand Rapids, Mich.: Zondervan Publishing House, 1981. This masterpiece chronologically harmonizes the gospel accounts of the life of Christ and integrates illuminating support from a variety of historical sources.

White, John. *The Cost of Commitment.* Downers Grove, Ill.: InterVarsity Press, 1976. This short but powerful book reveals the practical costs of making Jesus Lord of our lives and shows how those costs pale in light of the surpassing glory of living for the Savior.

Acknowledgments

Insight for Living is grateful for permission to quote from the following sources:

Lewis, C. S. *Mere Christianity.* Revised and enlarged. 1952. Reprint. London, England: William Collins Sons and Co., 1960.

——. *Surprised by Joy.* C. S. Lewis, 1955; renewed by Arthur Owen Barfield, executor of the estate of C. S. Lewis. Reprinted by permission of Harcourt Brace Jovanovich, Inc.

Lucado, Max. *No Wonder They Call Him the Savior.* Portland, Oreg.: Multnomah Press, 1986.

Insight for Living
Cassette Tapes
JESUS, OUR LORD

Who is Jesus? He is more than a Jewish carpenter reared in Nazareth . . . more than a good man who loved people . . . more than a martyr who died on a Roman cross.

He is *Jesus, Our Lord* . . . undiminished deity, yet true humanity—Savior from sin, promised Redeemer, someday to be acknowledged by all as King of Kings and Lord of Lords! Here are eight Bible-based messages about Him, each one easily understood by anyone who is interested in the most unique life ever lived on earth. And they are not only interesting, they are convincing. Jesus is indeed Lord!

			U.S.	Canada
JOL	CS	Cassette series—includes album cover	$23.75	$30.00
		Individual cassettes—include messages		
		A and B	5.00	6.35

These prices are effective as of February 1987 and are subject to change without notice.

JOL   1-A: *Jesus: His Existence Before Creation*
       John 8, Matthew 16
     B: *Jesus: A Birth Like None Other*
       Matthew 1, Luke 1

JOL   2-A: *Jesus: His God-Man Lifestyle*
       John 1, Philippians 2:5–7
     B: *Jesus: A Lamb Led to Slaughter*
       Isaiah 53, Matthew 26, John 19:17–30

JOL   3-A: *Jesus: Triumphant over the Grave*
       John 20
     B: *Jesus: Ascended and Seated in Heaven*
       Acts 1:1–11, Ephesians 1:18–23, Hebrews

JOL   4-A: *Jesus: His Promised Return*
       Matthew 24, 1 Thessalonians 4:13–18, 2 Peter 3:10–18
     B: *Jesus: He Is Lord*
       Ephesians 4

Ordering Information

U.S. ordering information: You are welcome to use our toll-free number (for Visa and MasterCard orders only) between the hours of 8:30 A.M. and 4:00 P.M., Pacific time, Monday through Friday. The number is **(800) 772-8888.** This number may be used anywhere in the continental United States except California, Hawaii, and Alaska. Orders from these areas are handled through our Sales Department at **(714) 870-9161.** We are unable to accept collect calls.

Your order will be processed promptly. We ask that you allow four to six weeks for delivery by fourth-class mail. If you wish your order to be shipped first-class, please add 10 percent of the total order cost (not including California sales tax) for shipping and handling.

Canadian ordering information: Your order will be processed promptly. We ask that you allow approximately four weeks for delivery by first-class mail to the U.S./Canadian border. All orders will be shipped from our office in Fullerton, California. For our listeners in British Columbia, a 7 percent sales tax must be added to the total of all tape orders (not including first-class postage). For further information, please contact our office at **(604) 272-5811.**

Payment options: We accept personal checks, money orders, Visa, and MasterCard in payment for materials ordered. Unfortunately, we are unable to offer invoicing or COD orders. If the amount of your check or money order is less than the amount of your purchase, your check will be returned so that you may place your order again with the correct amount. All orders must be paid in full before shipment can be made.

Returned checks: There is a $10 charge for any returned check (regardless of the amount of your order) to cover processing and invoicing.

Guarantee: Our tapes are guaranteed for ninety days against faulty performance or breakage due to a defect in the tape. For best results, please be sure your tape recorder is in good operating condition and is cleaned regularly.

Mail your order to one of the following addresses:

Insight for Living	Insight for Living Ministries
Sales Department	Post Office Box 2510
Post Office Box 4444	Vancouver, BC
Fullerton, CA 92634	Canada V6B 3W7

Quantity discounts and gift certificates are available upon request.

Overseas ordering information is provided on the reverse side of the order form.

Order Form

Please send me the following cassette tapes:

The current series: ☐ JOL CS Jesus, Our Lord

Individual cassettes: ☐ JOL 1 ☐ JOL 2 ☐ JOL 3 ☐ JOL 4

I am enclosing:

$ _____ To purchase the cassette series for $23.75 (in Canada $30.00*) which includes the album cover

$ _____ To purchase individual tapes at $5.00 each (in Canada $6.35*)

$ _____ Total of purchases

$ _____ If the order will be delivered in California, please add 6 percent sales tax

$ _____ U.S. residents please add 10 percent for first-class shipping and handling if desired

$ _____ *British Columbia residents please add 7 percent sales tax

$ _____ Canadian residents please add 6 percent for postage

$ _____ **Overseas residents please add appropriate postage** (See postage chart under "Overseas Ordering Information.")

$ _____ As a gift to the Insight for Living radio ministry for which a tax-deductible receipt will be issued

$ _____ **Total amount due (Please do not send cash.)**

Form of payment:

☐ Check or money order made payable to Insight for Living

☐ Credit card (Visa or MasterCard only)

If there is a balance: ☐ apply it as a donation ☐ please refund

---

Credit card purchases:

☐ Visa ☐ MasterCard number _____

Expiration date _____

Signature _____

We cannot process your credit card purchase without your signature.

Name _____

Address _____

_____

City _____

State/Province _____ Zip/Postal code _____

Country _____

Telephone ( ) _____ Radio station __ __ __ __

Should questions arise concerning your order, we may need to contact you.

Overseas Ordering Information

If you do not live in the United States or Canada, please note the following information. This will ensure efficient processing of your request.

Estimated time of delivery: We ask that you allow approximately twelve to sixteen weeks for delivery by surface mail. If you would like your order sent airmail, the length of delivery may be reduced. All orders will be shipped from our office in Fullerton, California.

Payment options: Due to fluctuating currency rates, we can accept only personal checks made payable in U.S. funds, international money orders, Visa, and MasterCard in payment for materials ordered. If the amount of your check or money order is less than the amount of your purchase, your check will be returned so that you may place your order again with the correct amount. All orders must be paid in full before shipment can be made.

Returned checks: There is a $10 charge for any returned check (regardless of the amount of your order) to cover processing and invoicing.

Postage and handling: Please add to the amount of purchase the postage cost for the service you desire. All orders must include postage based on the chart below.

Purchase Amount		Surface Postage	Airmail Postage
From	To	Percentage of Order	Percentage of Order
$ .01	$15.00	40%	75%
15.01	75.00	25%	45%
75.01	or more	15%	40%

Guarantee: Our tapes are guaranteed for ninety days against faulty performance or breakage due to a defect in the tape. For best results, please be sure your tape recorder is in good operating condition and is cleaned regularly.

Mail your order or inquiry to the following address:

Insight for Living
Sales Department
Post Office Box 4444
Fullerton, CA 92634

Quantity discounts and gift certificates are available upon request.